W9-AHC-473

The Manager's Pocket Guide to

DIVERSITY MANAGEMENT

Dr. Edward E. Hubbard

HRD PRESS, Inc.
Amherst, Massachusetts

Published by:
HRD Press
22 Amherst Road
Amherst, MA 01002-9709
800-822-2801 (U.S. and Canada)
413-253-3488
413-253-3490 (Fax)
www.hrdpress.com

ISBN 0-87425-761-1

Cover design by Eileen Klockars
Editorial services by Sally Farnham
Typeset by Pracharak Technologies (P) Ltd, Madras, India

TABLE OF CONTENTS

PREFACE

Why should you concern yourself with effective diversity management? In the past, many managers answered this question by saying that it was the "right thing to do," or that they were seeing more and more people who didn't look like themselves in the workforce, or that they felt they had to meet the organization's requirement for working with diverse groups. However, today's managers know that without effective diversity management capability, the strength of the organization is in jeopardy. Being effective at managing a diverse workforce helps lift morale, improve processes, bring access to new segments of the marketplace, enhance productivity, and improve the financial bottom line of the organization. In essence, it is good for business.

This pocket guide is designed to help you build diversity management skills to create a high-performing work environment. It should be used as an interactive workbook to test your skills; teach or reinforce diversity concepts and knowledge; and provide tools, processes, and techniques to use a diverse workforce to improve organizational performance. Whether you are launching a new diversity initiative, building a diverse work team, or planning a new, innovative product launch, you will find the information in this guidebook an invaluable asset for managerial and leadership development.

The true measure of the effectiveness of this book will be determined in large part by your willingness to read the information, try the exercises, internalize the information, and build on your learning. The first chapter will help you assess your skills in managing diversity and explain its importance to business performance. The next four chapters will help you learn

diversity definitions, theories, and concepts that serve as a
basic diversity learning foundation. The remaining chapters
provide workplace applications for key diversity-related initiatives, strategies for boosting productivity, approaches for managing the diversity change process, and building blocks for a
personal action plan.

As you read this guide, you will gain awareness, knowledge,
skills, tools, and techniques that will help you improve your
ability to manage diversity. This guide will help you test your
diversity leadership awareness and knowledge, save management time, help you navigate difficult situations, provide
techniques for teamwork, and improve your interpersonal
effectiveness. In short, it is designed for anyone who would
like to improve their personal diversity management and
leadership performance as well as the performance of their
organization.

ACKNOWLEDGMENTS

This book is dedicated to my loving wife, Myra. She continues to be my inspiration and source of strength. In addition, no one creates a book like this without the direct or indirect help of many people. They include all of the many scholars quoted and/or used as a resource in this guidebook and many others too numerous to mention—I thank you all. I would also like to thank Chris Hunter and the staff at HRD Press for their patience and tenacity in seeing this project through. And finally, this book is dedicated to all of the current and future champions of diversity; I hope that it helps you and others realize the truly unlimited potential of a diverse workforce and the importance of your diversity management contribution!

Chapter 1
Assessing Your Skills

The purpose of this chapter is to provide you with information to help assess your current level of skill in managing diversity. Although you may be eager to get right to work learning and developing your skills, the best place to start is with an assessment of your current skill level to indicate your starting point.

The Managing Diversity Profile

Before you begin reading this pocket guide, take a minute to complete Exercise 1-1, the Managing Diversity Profile (adapted from the comprehensive 360° Diversity Leadership Competency Profile from Hubbard & Hubbard, Inc.). This self-assessment examines your current level of skill for managing diversity and provides you feedback on six key competencies for managing diversity.

Exercise 1-1. Managing Diversity Profile
by Dr. Edward E. Hubbard

Directions: This profile is designed to help you examine your diversity management skills. We hope that you will be frank and honest in rating these items and that you indicate your rating based on what you believe to be true about how you respond in a diverse work environment. You should indicate your rating by placing a *single* checkmark on the number in

the brackets next to the appropriate term that best reflects
"*what you actually do*"—for example, [✓] Never, or
[✓] Rarely, or [✓] Sometimes, or [✓] Often, or [✓] Usually, or
[✓] Almost Always. Only **one** checkmark should be indicated
for each item.

Section One

1. Communicates a diversity vision for organizational success
   that sparks excitement in others.
   [1] Never   [2] Rarely   [3] Sometimes   [4] Often
   [5] Usually [6] Almost Always

2. Encourages managers to promote and explain the diversity
   vision.
   [1] Never   [2] Rarely   [3] Sometimes   [4] Often
   [5] Usually [6] Almost Always

3. Regularly measures your own diversity progress and the
   progress of your staff toward the diversity vision.
   [1] Never   [2] Rarely   [3] Sometimes   [4] Often
   [5] Usually [6] Almost Always

4. Asks employees for their input to the diversity vision.
   [1] Never   [2] Rarely   [3] Sometimes   [4] Often
   [5] Usually [6] Almost Always

Section Two

5. Communicates easily with people of diverse backgrounds.
   [1] Never   [2] Rarely   [3] Sometimes   [4] Often
   [5] Usually [6] Almost Always

6. Speaks effectively in front of diverse groups.
   [1] Never   [2] Rarely   [3] Sometimes   [4] Often
   [5] Usually [6] Almost Always

7. Gives constructive feedback effectively to all groups
   regardless of race, gender, or other diverse
   characteristics.
   [1] Never   [2] Rarely   [3] Sometimes   [4] Often
   [5] Usually [6] Almost Always

8. Listens to feedback from diverse groups without becoming
   defensive.
   [1] Never   [2] Rarely   [3] Sometimes   [4] Often
   [5] Usually [6] Almost Always

Section Three

9. Discusses diversity as a strength in this organization.
   [1] Never   [2] Rarely   [3] Sometimes   [4] Often
   [5] Usually [6] Almost Always

10. Gives people of diverse backgrounds equal opportunity for
    training, promotion, etc.
    [1] Never   [2] Rarely   [3] Sometimes   [4] Often
    [5] Usually [6] Almost Always

11. Seeks to understand the cultural norms and practices of
    groups other than your own.
    [1] Never   [2] Rarely   [3] Sometimes   [4] Often
    [5] Usually [6] Almost Always

12. Makes use of the diverse talents of people in work assign-
    ments, decision making, etc.
    [1] Never   [2] Rarely   [3] Sometimes   [4] Often
    [5] Usually [6] Almost Always

Section Four

13. Consults with diverse groups to find innovative ways to make change happen.
    [1] Never   [2] Rarely   [3] Sometimes   [4] Often
    [5] Usually   [6] Almost Always

14. Gets input from employees about changes that will have an impact on them.
    [1] Never   [2] Rarely   [3] Sometimes   [4] Often
    [5] Usually   [6] Almost Always

15. Works to resolve diverse work group issues related to impending changes.
    [1] Never   [2] Rarely   [3] Sometimes   [4] Often
    [5] Usually   [6] Almost Always

16. Keeps people informed during the process of change.
    [1] Never   [2] Rarely   [3] Sometimes   [4] Often
    [5] Usually   [6] Almost Always

Section Five

17. Solicits input from groups regardless of race, gender, or other characteristics.
    [1] Never   [2] Rarely   [3] Sometimes   [4] Often
    [5] Usually   [6] Almost Always

18. Manages more like a colleague than as a boss.
    [1] Never   [2] Rarely   [3] Sometimes   [4] Often
    [5] Usually   [6] Almost Always

19. Shares accountability with diverse groups equitably.
    [1] Never   [2] Rarely   [3] Sometimes   [4] Often
    [5] Usually [6] Almost Always

20. Rewards diverse groups for their contributions in a fair manner.
    [1] Never   [2] Rarely   [3] Sometimes   [4] Often
    [5] Usually [6] Almost Always

Section Six

21. Delegates responsibility fully to those qualified to do the work regardless of race, gender, or other characteristics.
    [1] Never   [2] Rarely   [3] Sometimes   [4] Often
    [5] Usually [6] Almost Always

22. Works to customize training needs to fit diverse work group members.
    [1] Never   [2] Rarely   [3] Sometimes   [4] Often
    [5] Usually [6] Almost Always

23. Counsels and mentors diverse work group members on their interests, preferences, and careers.
    [1] Never   [2] Rarely   [3] Sometimes   [4] Often
    [5] Usually [6] Almost Always

24. Demonstrates valuing diversity through his/her own actions.
    [1] Never   [2] Rarely   [3] Sometimes   [4] Often
    [5] Usually [6] Almost Always

Scoring Process

Each item has a possible maximum score of 6 points.

Step One: Enter the score for each item in the Profile Scoring Grid on page 7 using the following numbers for each response (for example, if you placed a checkmark in the brackets next to the term "Usually," then Usually = 5 points):
[1] Never   [2] Rarely   [3] Sometimes   [4] Often
[5] Usually [6] Almost Always

Step Two: After indicating the numerical points in the left-hand side of the Profile Scoring Grid, add your scores horizontally, enter your score under "Competency," and draw a "bar" to the appropriate box under the Total Score Graph based on the total points you tallied. See sample below (5 pts. + 6 pts. + 2 pts. + 1 pt. = 14 points):

Sample

Profile Scoring Grid		Total Score Graph							
Items	Competency	1–4	5–6	7–10	11–12	13–16	17–18	19–22	23–24
[1] [2] [3] [4] 5 6 2 1	*Champion for Diversity* Max: 24 pts. Score:	██	██	██	██				

Profile Scoring Grid					Total Score Graph							
Items				Competency	1–4	5–6	7–10	11–12	13–16	17–18	19–22	23–24
1	2	3	4	**Champion for Diversity** *Max: 24 pts. Score:*								
5	6	7	8	**Communicates Across Cultures** *Max: 24 pts. Score:*								
9	10	11	12	**Diversity Orientation** *Max: 24 pts. Score:*								
13	14	15	16	**Leads Change** *Max: 24 pts. Score:*								
17	18	19	20	**Empowers Others to Act** *Max: 24 pts. Score:*								
21	22	23	24	**Develops Others** *Max: 24 pts. Score:*								
				Overall Profile Score: *Sum of all Competency Totals/6 Max: 24 pts. Score:*								

Your Overall Profile Score is the sum totals of all competencies (Champion for Diversity, Communicates Across Cultures, Diversity Orientation, Leads Change, Empowers Others to Act, and Develops Others) **divided by 6**. Calculate your Overall Profile Score and draw a "bar" to the appropriate box on the right under the Total Score Graph, based on the total points.

The interpretation of your Overall Profile Score is shown below:

Excellent: (20 to 24)

Congratulations! You have successfully integrated the diversity management competencies into your style and the way you interact with others. This makes it possible for you and the organization to strategically capitalize on employee differences. You should try to expand your lessons learned as personal development and help others in your organization who may not be as far along as you.

Very Good: (17 to 19)

You are making progress and have all the ingredients for even greater success. Focus on the areas that received the lower scores and address them.

Average: (15 to 16)

You have some core strengths but there are areas for growth and improvement. Review the areas that received the lowest scores and discuss them with your manager and/or a peer coach/mentor who is effective at managing a diverse work-force. At the same time, also look at one or two areas that received the highest scores and think about ways to sustain these strengths.

Poor—Potential Problems Ahead: (14 and below)

You may already be running into problems managing your diverse workforce. Pick one or two key competency areas that received low scores on the assessment, and focus your efforts using the skills outlined in this pocket guide. Consider obtaining a peer coach/mentor who is effective at managing a diverse workforce to help you bring your skills to a high-performing level. Attend managing diversity workshops and other developmental activities for improvement.

To get you started, use the **Managing Diversity Profile Action Plan Start-up Toolkit** in Figure 1-1, which is packed with recommended activities, suggestions, and tools you can use to enhance your skills in each area.

Figure 1-1. Managing Diversity Profile Action Plan Start-Up Toolkit

If you want to build skills to. . .	Actions you can take include. . .	Resources you can use include. . .
Become a Champion for Diversity	❖ Make diversity not just a business strategy, but a way of life. Demonstrate a zero-tolerance policy toward any type of discrimination (age, race, sex, class, sexual orientation, physical ability, etc.). ❖ Personally communicate support for diversity internally and externally using all media. ❖ Hold managers accountable for communicating and implementing the diversity vision. ❖ Meet with employees who are different and share perspectives.	❖ *Diversity making it work: Interview with Dr. Edward E. Hubbard* [Film] (1999). American Media Films. Produced by Ash-Quarry Productions, Learning A La Carte series. Available from Hubbard & Hubbard, Inc., 707-763-8380. ❖ Gardenswartz, L., & Rowe, A. (1993). *Managing diversity: A complete desk reference and planning guide.* Homewood, IL: Business One Irwin.

	❖ Participate in a coaching event where senior management is required to attend, where teams are created with a diverse range of people, and coaching is integrated into daily tasks. ❖ Select diversity-related issues to discuss as a topic at town hall meetings, staff meetings, forums, etc.	❖ Book: *Voices of diversity.* ❖ Thomas, R. R. (1999). *Building a house for diversity.* New York: AMACOM.
Effectively Communicate Across Cultures	❖ Become aware of your own reaction to change, as well as your ability to interact with others who are different from you, your adaptability to alternative solutions and unstructured situations, your mental flexibility, and your intellectual curiosity. ❖ Choose a colleague to meet with regularly who also wishes to manage with more sensitivity to differences. Share goals, set milestones, and report on progress.	

(continued)

If you want to build skills to. . .	Actions you can take include. . .	Resources you can use include. . .
Effectively Communicate Across Cultures (concluded)	❖ Participate and speak at events in organizations/events where you are different from others in attendance. ❖ Publicize diversity success stories and show the business relevance.	❖ Kuga, L. A. (1996). *Communicating in a diverse workplace.* Irvine, CA: Richard Chang & Associates. Available through Hubbard & Hubbard, Inc., 707-763-8380.
Develop a Diversity Orientation	❖ Seek out and build relationships with people who are different than you in race, gender, ethnicity, physical ability, sexual orientation, age, etc. ❖ Learn about differences in the workforce through reading, attending workshops, fostering relationships with people who are different, and participating in activities that are diversity related.	❖ Fernandez, J. P. (1991). *Managing a diverse workforce: Regaining the competitive edge.* Lexington, MA: Lexington Books. ❖ Diversity Leadership Competency Profile

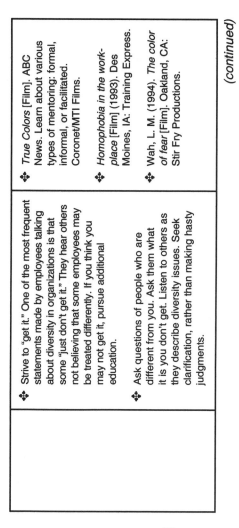

❖ Strive to "get it." One of the most frequent statements made by employees talking about diversity in organizations is that some "just don't get it." They hear others not believing that some employees may be treated differently. If you think you may not get it, pursue additional education.

❖ Ask questions of people who are different from you. Ask them what it is you don't get. Listen to others as they describe diversity issues. Seek clarification, rather than making hasty judgments.

❖ *True Colors* [Film]. ABC News. Learn about various types of mentoring: formal, informal, or facilitated. Coronet/MTI Films.

❖ *Homophobia in the work-place* [Film] (1993). Des Moines, IA: Training Express.

❖ Wah, L. M. (1994). *The color of fear* [Film]. Oakland, CA: Stir Fry Productions.

(continued)

If you want to build skills to...	Actions you can take include...	Resources you can use include...
Lead Change	❖ Offer to coordinate or participate in an event that educates others about a specific diversity topic or view. ❖ Volunteer for a tough diversity assignment in your workplace or community to help find solutions to meet the needs of a diverse population. Be proactive in looking for chances to stretch yourself and learn something. ❖ Begin a staff meeting with the following question: "What actions did you take last week to utilize the strength of our diversity to make our performance even better this week?" Persist in asking this question for at least three meetings in a row so that everyone knows you're serious about diversity and its importance for performance and change. By the way, be prepared to answer this same question for yourself at each meeting.	❖ Hubbard, E. E., Ph.D. (1997). *Measuring diversity results.* Petaluma, CA: Global Insight Publishing. Available through Hubbard & Hubbard, Inc., 707-763-8380. ❖ *Harvard business review on managing diversity* (2001). Cambridge, MA: Harvard Business School Press. ❖ Thomas, R. R. (1999). *Building a house for diversity.* New York: AMACOM. Available through Hubbard & Hubbard, Inc., 707-763-8380.

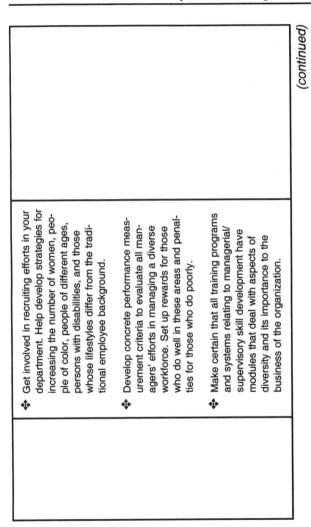

❖ Get involved in recruiting efforts in your department. Help develop strategies for increasing the number of women, people of color, people of different ages, persons with disabilities, and those whose lifestyles differ from the traditional employee background.

❖ Develop concrete performance measurement criteria to evaluate all managers' efforts in managing a diverse workforce. Set up rewards for those who do well in these areas and penalties for those who do poorly.

❖ Make certain that all training programs and systems relating to managerial/supervisory skill development have modules that deal with aspects of diversity and its importance to the business of the organization.

(continued)

If you want to build skills to. . .	Actions you can take include. . .	Resources you can use include. . .
Empower Others to Act	❖ Find ways to increase interactions among people who need to work more effectively together. Teamwork and trust can only be built when people interact informally as well as formally. Establish easily accessible, common meeting areas that encourage people to interact. Put the coffee pot or the popcorn maker in a location between groups that should talk to each other. ❖ Ask other people from other parts of the organization to attend your regular staff meetings. ❖ Schedule a lunch for two or more groups that don't spend much time face to face.	❖ Simons, G. (1994). *Working together: How to become more effective in a multicultural environment.* Menlo Park, CA: Crisp Publications. ❖ Myers, S. G. (1996). *Team building for diverse work groups.* Irvine, CA: Richard Chang & Associates. Available through Hubbard & Hubbard, Inc., 707-763-8380.

Develop Others	
❖ Develop effective listening and delegation skills.	❖ Managing Work Expectations Profile—A self-assessment, self-scoring instrument. Inscape Products, distributed by Hubbard & Hubbard, Inc., 707-763-8380.
❖ Integrate diversity into your business plan. Review Individual Development Plan (IDP) actions for completeness and talent utilization, and provide required support.	
❖ Create a random spot check procedure to examine Individual Development Plans (IDPs) for women, people of color, and any other underrepresented group.	❖ O'Mara, J. *101 actions you can take to value and manage diversity.* Available from Hubbard & Hubbard, Inc., 707-763-8380.
❖ Inventory your employees' educational background, work experiences, job knowledge, specialized skills, number of opportunities they have had to gain development, participation in special skill-building assignments, the amount of cross-training they have received, etc.	

(continued)

If you want to build skills to. . .	Actions you can take include. . .	Resources you can use include. . .
Develop Others (concluded)	❖ Train managers and direct reports in effective career planning, development, and coaching skills when working with others who are different from yourself. Spend time identifying their specific roles and responsibilities and how you will measure their progress.	❖ Tannen, D. (1995). *Talking 9 to 5: Men and women in the workplace.* New York: Harper Collins.

Managing and leading in a diverse work environment, in general, requires that you follow the ten guidelines in Figure 1-2.

Figure 1-2. Ten Guidelines for Managing and Leading in a Diverse Work Environment*

✓	Activity
	Search out challenging opportunities to utilize diversity to change, grow, innovate, and improve.
	Experiment, take risks, learn from the accompanying mistakes, and seek feedback.
	Envision an inclusive, strategically anchored future using diversity.
	Enlist others in a common vision by incorporating and appealing to their values, interests, hopes, and dreams.
	Foster collaboration by promoting cooperative goal setting and building trust.
	Strengthen people by giving power away, providing choices, developing competence, assigning critical tasks, and offering visible support.
	Set the example by seeking cultural knowledge and behaving in ways that are consistent with shared values.
	Achieve small wins that promote consistent progress and build commitment by sharing measurable diversity results.
	Recognize individual contributions to the success of every project in the manner consistent with the contributor's needs and wants.
	Celebrate diverse work team accomplishments regularly.

* Adapted from Kouzes, J. M., & Posner, B. Z. *Ten commandments of leadership.*

The Impact of Diversity on Business Performance

In profit-making organizations, maximizing the difference between revenues and costs optimizes performance. This same goal exists in many non-profit organizations, except that the result is called surplus instead of profits. The question therefore is "How is workforce diversity and its management related to revenues, costs, or both?" To answer this question, we can explore several concepts and strategies that illustrate the impact of diversity on business performance. These concepts and strategies include items such as marketing strategies, problem-solving strategies, and creativity and innovation that can be viewed as important factors in revenue generation.

Marketing Strategies

We live and work in an increasingly global marketplace, making diversity a crucial issue. Whether your business includes marketing financial services, computers, telecommunications products, social services, health care equipment, manufacturing processes, engineering expertise, or the like, expertise in addressing a diverse customer market will be essential to your success. For example, an automobile manufacturer in Japan cannot afford to ignore the fact that nearly half of all new car buyers in the United States are women. This is true regardless of the gender makeup of car buyers in Japan. Likewise, no reasonable person in the consumer-goods industry can afford to ignore the fact that roughly a quarter of the world's population is Chinese, and immigration to the United States from mostly Asian and Latin American countries is occurring at a rate of more than one million people per year.

In the United States today, Asians, African Americans, and Hispanics combined to collectively represent nearly $1 trillion annually in consumer spending. The Selig Center for Economic Growth's (from the University of Georgia Terry School of Management) estimates and projections of buying power for 1990–2007 show that minorities—African Americans, Asians Native Americans, and Hispanics—definitely share in this success and together wield formidable economic clout. As these groups increase in number and purchasing power, their growing shares of the U.S. consumer market draw avid attention from producers, retailers, and service providers alike.

The buying power data presented here and differences in spending by race and/or ethnicity suggest that one general advertisement, product, or service geared for all consumers increasingly misses many potentially profitable market opportunities. As the U.S. consumer market becomes more diverse, advertising, products, and media must be tailored to each market segment. With this in mind, new entrepreneurs, established businesses, marketing specialists, economic development organizations, and chambers of commerce now seek estimates of the buying power of the nation's major racial and ethnic minority groups. The Selig Center projects that the nation's total buying power will rise from $4.3 trillion in 1990 to $7 trillion in 2000, to $7.6 trillion in 2002, and to $9.9 trillion in 2007. The percentage increase for the 17-year period of 1990–2007 is 130.8 percent, which far exceeds cumulative inflation. The spending habits of racial and ethnic minority groups accounts for a great deal of this substantial growth.

Buying Power Statistics by Race

In 2007, the combined buying power of African Americans, Asians, and Native Americans will be more than triple its 1990 level of $453 billion and will total almost $1.4 trillion, a gain of $912 billion or 201 percent. In 2007, African Americans will account for 62 percent of combined spending, or $853 billion. Over this 17-year period, the percentage gains in minority buying power vary considerably by race, from a gain of 287 percent for Asians to 197 percent for Native Americans to 170 percent for African Americans. All of these target markets will grow much faster than the white market, where buying power will increase by only 112 percent.

The combined buying power of these three groups will account for 13.8 percent of the nation's total buying power in 2007, up from 10.6 percent in 1990. This 3.2 percent gain in combined market share amounts to an additional $316 billion in buying power in 2007. The market share claimed by a targeted group of consumers is important because the higher their market share, the lower the average cost of reaching a potential buyer in the group. Managers in organizations must possess effective multi-cultural marketing savvy to meet specific needs of a diverse marketplace and to affect buying behavior.

If an organization plans to sell or deliver goods and services in a diverse marketplace, it must be fully capable of effectively using its diverse workforce in key strategic ways. For instance, it is important from a public relations standpoint to be viewed as a company that is known for managing and utilizing its diverse workforce assets well. There are a number of well-publicized ratings for "The Best Company for Working Women and Working Mothers," "The Most Admired Company," and "The Top 50 Companies for Women and Minorities." This fuels a public relations climate where workforce talent and consumers make choices about the organizations they would work for and buy from. This line of thinking is also supported by a study of stock price responses to publicity that changed either positively or negatively on an organization's ability to manage diversity. The authors of this study found that announcements of awards for exemplary efforts resulted in significant positive changes in stock prices, while announcements of discrimination suits resulted in significant negative changes in stock prices (Wright, Ferris, Hiller, & Kroll, 1995).

In addition, an organization can gain a great deal from the insights of its diverse workforce to understand the cultural effects of buying decisions and to map strategies to respond to them. Depending on the product or service delivered by the organization, many employees may also represent part of the firm's customer base. A good reputation inside the organization can help product and service sales outside the organization. Another key marketing strategy includes tapping employee network or resource groups. They can be an excellent resource for focus groups, feedback, and ideas for honing the organization's reach into diverse marketplace opportunities.

Problem Solving

Revenue increases can also show up due to improvements in diverse work team problem solving and decision making. Diverse work teams have a broader and richer base of experience to draw on in solving organizations' problems and issues. The presence of minority views creates higher levels of critical analysis of assumptions and implications of decisions. In addition, it also generates an increase in the number of alternatives from which the group chooses. Simply mixing people together who are culturally different does not necessarily result in diverse work groups that execute beneficial problem solving. The improved outcomes heavily depend on a diversity-competent manager who uses key diversity management behaviors.

In one study, researchers found that properly managed and trained diverse work teams produced scores that were six times higher than homogeneous teams. Researchers also found that it is important how a diverse team uses its diversity. For example, those diverse teams that recognized and utilized their diversity had higher productivity. And even when the team was diverse, if that diversity was not used effectively, it, in some cases, caused process problems that resulted in lower team productivity. The essential variable is the ability to *effectively manage and utilize the team's diversity.*

Creativity and Innovation

Creativity and innovation can be vital to an organization's ability to perform. New product introductions, advertising, process re-engineering, and quality improvements are examples where these skills are required. Diverse work teams have also been found to promote improved creativity and innovation that generates revenue. In her book *The Change Masters* (1983), Rosabeth Moss Kanter notes that highly innovative companies have done a better job of eradicating racism, sexism, and classism; tend to have workforces that are more race and gender diverse; and take deliberate steps to create heterogeneous work teams with the objective of bringing that diversity to bear on organizational problems and issues.

As you read this guide, you will gain awareness, knowledge, skills, tools, and techniques that will help you improve your ability to manage diversity. This guide will help you test your awareness and knowledge, save time, facilitate difficult situations, provide techniques for teamwork and improve your interpersonal effectiveness. Now that you have had an opportunity to assess your skills, you are ready to gain a better understanding of requirements for managing diversity. Often the best place to start is with a definition of diversity, which we will explore in the next chapter.

References

Hubbard, E. E. (2001). *Diversity leadership competency profile.* Petaluma, CA: Global Insights Publishing.

Hubbard, E. E. (1999, 2003). *Managing diversity profile.* Petaluma, CA: Global Insights Publishing.

Hubbard, E. E. (2002). *Techniques for managing a diverse workforce.* Petaluma, CA: Global Insights Publishing.

Kouzes, J. M. & Posner, B. Z. (2001). *Leadership practices inventory.* San Francisco, CA: Jossey-Bass, Pfeiffer.

Moss Kanter, R. (1983). *The change masters.* New York: Simon & Schuster.

O'Mara, J. (1999). *101 actions you can take to value and manage diversity.* Castro Valley, CA: O'Mara & Associates.

Wright, P., Ferris, S. P., Hiller, J. S., & Kroll, M. (1995). Competitiveness through management of diversity: Effects on stock price valuation. *Academy of Management Journal,* Vol. 38, n1, pp. 272–287.

Chapter 2
What Is Diversity?

Definition and Terms

Any useful discussion of the topic of diversity must start with a fundamental clarification of the term. The term *diversity* itself has a number of different interpretations. *Diversity* can be defined as a **"collective mixture characterized by differences and similarities that are applied in pursuit of organizational objectives."** *Diversity management* then can be defined as **"the process of planning for, organizing, directing, and supporting these collective mixtures in a way that adds a measurable difference to organizational performance."**

Diversity and its mixtures can be organized into four interdependent and sometimes overlapping aspects: Workforce diversity, behavioral diversity, structural diversity, and business diversity.

Workforce diversity encompasses group and situational identities of the organization's employees (i.e., gender, race, ethnicity, religion, sexual orientation, physical ability, age, family status, economic background and status, and geographical background and status). It also includes changes in the labor market demographics.

Behavioral diversity encompasses work styles, thinking styles, learning styles, communication styles, aspirations, beliefs/value systems as well as changes in the attitudes and expectation on the part of employees.

Structural diversity encompasses interactions across functions, across organizational levels in the hierarchy, across divisions, between parent companies and subsidiaries, and across organizations engaged in strategic alliances and cooperative ventures. As organizations attempt to become more flexible, less layered, more team-based, and more multi- and cross-functional, measuring this type of diversity will require more attention.

Business diversity encompasses the expansion and segmentation of customer markets, the diversification of products and services offered, and the variety of operating environments in which organizations work and compete (i.e., legal and regulatory context, labor market realities, community and societal expectations/relationships, business cultures and norms). Increasing competitive pressures, globalization, rapid advances in product technologies, changing demographics in the customer bases both within domestic markets and across borders, and shifts in business/government relationships all signal a need to measure an organization's response and impact on business diversity.

As you can see, diversity is a mosaic of mixtures that includes everyone, representing their differences and similarities, and the variety of processes, systems, and aspects of the global environment in which the organization must respond. An organization's inherent bias about diversity can cloud the definition and is often reflected in the way it is positioned and defined by executives and managers. When executives and managers have not internalized the important message that diversity includes everyone, their comments frequently imply that "white males need not apply." In many organizations, diversity has been positioned to focus on women and people of color, therefore a "diverse person" in such an organization cannot be a white man.

Some organizations use diversity as a shorthand for a variety of characteristics such as learning style, individual thinking style, and so on, but often leave out issues of differences involving race, gender, age, physical abilities, and sexual orientation. In any event, the definitions are less comprehensive than they should be to address the real opportunities and complex issues that diversity offers. Given today's workplace and marketplace challenges, with fierce competition for talent and market share, market pressures for responsiveness, etc., diversity offers many opportunities and advantages. The entire organization must clearly understand what diversity and diversity management truly mean and realize that diversity involves everyone.

Primary and Secondary Dimensions

A fundamental error that some people make is thinking diversity is synonymous with the word *culture*. They think diversity focuses on "what Hispanics do in their culture" or "what women want." This approach is inherently flawed because it reinforces stereotypes, which those who truly value diversity are trying to eliminate.

People come in a variety of shapes, sizes, and colors. This variety is what differentiates us from one another. While we share the important dimensions of humanness with all members of our species, there are biological and environmental differences that separate and distinguish us as individuals and groups. It is this vast array of physical and cultural differences that constitutes the spectrum of human diversity.

Since people are different, the definition of diversity must include important human characteristics that impact an individual's values, opportunities, and perceptions of themselves and others at work and that highlight how individuals aggregate into

29

larger subgroups based on shared characteristics. Using these criteria, a workplace definition would, at bare minimum, include

❖ Age

❖ Ethnicity

❖ Gender

❖ Mental/physical abilities and characteristics

❖ Race

❖ Sexual orientation

These six differences are called *core* or *primary* dimensions of diversity because they exert an important impact on our early socialization and a powerful, sustained impact throughout every stage of life. These six dimensions represent properties and characteristics that constitute the core of our diverse identities. All individuals have a variety of dimensions of diversity through which they experience the world and by which they are defined. At the core of each of us, there is at least a minimum of these six dimensions.

Beyond the six *primary* dimensions, there are several *secondary* dimensions that play an important role in shaping our values, expectations, and experiences as well. These include

❖ Communication style

❖ Education

❖ Family status

❖ Military experience

❖ Organizational role and level

- ❖ Religion
- ❖ First language
- ❖ Geographic location
- ❖ Income
- ❖ Work experience
- ❖ Work style

Like the core dimensions, these secondary dimensions share certain characteristics. Generally, they are more variable in nature, less visible to others around us, and more variable in the degree of influence they exert on our individual lives. Many secondary dimensions contain an element of control or choice. Because we acquire, discard, and modify these dimensions, their power is less constant and more individualized than is true for the core dimensions. Yet despite the fact that these dimensions have less life-long influence, most individuals are more conscious of their impact at a given point in time than they are regarding primary dimensions. Usually, it is easier to see the connection of these secondary dimensions and events in someone's life (e.g., their first language might influence their communication style, their education level might influence their organizational role and level, etc.).

Often people refer to primary dimensions as those they are able to see. They include things people know about us before we open our mouths, because they are physically visible (except sexual orientation). When people feel they are being stereotyped based on primary dimensions, they can become sensitive about it. People are usually less sensitive about secondary dimensions, because they are elements we have made a choice on or have the power to change. We also have the choice of whether or not to disclose information about secondary dimensions; we can conceal it if we like.

Think about which dimensions have the most impact on you as a person. The primary dimensions are important; nonetheless, we are greatly influenced by where we live, whether we are married or not, and our financial status. The primary and secondary dimensions help us perceive each other's uniqueness far beyond our culture or communication style. They help us begin to define who we really are as unique individuals.

An example of these primary and secondary dimensions of diversity is shown in Figure 2-1.

Figure 2-1. Primary and Secondary Dimensions of Diversity

One of the major areas of difficulty in dealing with diversity is how people react to difference. In most cases, peoples' responses have already been imprinted since early childhood, based on a wide range of influences. When individuals start to realize the extent to which these influences have shaped their perceptions, awareness begins. Awareness then leads to greater understanding and, ultimately, the potential to build a positive environment. Awareness also opens a window of opportunity for you and the organization to focus on a new, more effective path. The challenge for you as a manager of today's workplace is to harness the strength of this diversity, nurture it, and use it to mold a productive workplace that the organization needs and desires.

A diverse workplace is inevitable, but the benefits of diversity are not inevitable unless that diversity is used in a way that adds a measurable difference to organizational performance. The environment within the organization will determine if the benefits of diversity are realized. Specific steps must be taken to create an environment where all employees feel welcome, feel valued for what they bring to the organization, and feel that their talents are being utilized. While each diversity dimension adds a layer of complexity, it is the dynamic interaction among all dimensions of diversity that influences a person's self-image, values, opportunities, and expectations—and, from an organizational standpoint, offers a tremendous opportunity for improved performance and competitive advantage.

Diversity Statistics Quiz

The statistical demographics of today's workplace will change from region to region, and occupation to occupation. The only constant is that we continue to develop and change through the individual contributions of a vast combination of cultures, languages, and abilities, all working together to achieve success. This requires managers to be aware of and sensitive to differences in the workplace and to use that knowledge without reinforcing negative stereotypes. What's your level of knowledge of diversity? The quiz below will help you gain information regarding changes related to diversity and explore the possible implications and impact on your organization. Simply complete the worksheet in Exercise 2-1. Answers to the quiz can be found in Figure 2-3 at the end of the chapter.

Exercise 2-1. Diversity Statistics Quiz

1. By the year 2020, what will be the estimated percentage of females in the workforce? _____%

2. Of the 8.7 million immigrants who arrived in the United States between 1980 and 1990, what percentage have college degrees? _____% What percentage of U.S. natives have college degrees? _____%

3. In the United States, what percentage of male executives under age 40 are fathers?_____% What percentage of female executives under age 40 are mothers? _____%

4. What are the two most racially and ethnically diverse states in the United States? _____ The two least? _____

5. How many people indicated they were "multi-racial" in the 2000 Census? Select a letter:
   (a) 1 million (b) 20 million (c) 12 million (d) 7 million

6. Fill in the blanks: Women make up _____ percent of all shoppers in the United States; they spend _____ cents of every dollar.

7. By the year 2050, what percent of the total U.S. population will Asians, Hispanics, African Americans, and other non-white groups represent? _____ %

8. What demographic group represents the fastest growing customer base in the United States? _____

9. What are the top six frequently cited barriers to advancement listed by women in the workplace? _____

10. Fill in the blank: One out of _____ African-American households makes more than $50,000 per year.

Interpreting Your Answers

As you review your answers to this diversity quiz, ask yourself the following questions:

❖ What questions were the most difficult? Why?

❖ Which of your answers were the most surprising? Why?

❖ Which demographics will potentially have the most impact on your organization? Why?

❖ What are the most significant implications of these changing demographics?

Workplace Trends

There are a number of studies that have followed the changing mosaic of America. Two of the most widely publicized studies were commissioned by the U.S. Department of Labor and conducted by the Hudson Institute: "Workforce 2000" in 1987, and ten years later "Workforce 2020" in 1997. According to these studies, the most significant trends in the U.S. population are

❖ Decreasing percentage of Caucasians

❖ Increasing percentage of people of color

❖ Decreasing birth rates

❖ Increasing percentages of people in their middle and older years

These trends translate into significant changes in the workforce composition, from more homogeneous to heterogeneous as shown in Figure 2-2.

Figure 2-2. Changing Trend from a Homogeneous Workforce to a More Heterogeneous Workforce

Homogeneous	Heterogeneous
❖ White male	❖ Women and minorities
❖ 29 years old	❖ 40+ years old
❖ Married with children	❖ Variety of lifestyles
❖ Less than 12 years of education	❖ 12+ years of education

Because of these changes in the workforce, organizations must be prepared to deal with

❖ An equal balance of men and women

❖ Shrinking numbers of whites and increasing numbers of people of color

❖ Most *new entrants* to the workforce will be women or people of color (over 85 percent in the 21st century)

❖ A shortage of *new entrants* in the workforce under age 24

❖ An increasing percentage of people aged 35 to 55 and older

The bottom line is that the workplace of the past no longer exists and hasn't for quite some time. It is not like past years when the typical workplace was made up of a homogeneous group of married white men who were 29 years old, married, with less than 12 years of education. During that time, most of them had wives who were "stay-at-home" mothers to care for the children. Compare this with today's reality of a workplace rich with diverse people from all walks of life, backgrounds, values, and ways of perceiving the world. Nonetheless, many organizations are structured for operation around the "old homogeneous model" that diminishes their ability to grow and ultimately to compete in a global marketplace.

People in the homogeneous workplace naturally created an American work environment that was appropriate for people who were present in the workforce at that time and who had similar backgrounds. When the organizational structure reflected the needs, backgrounds, and values of those who were in it, the system worked well for getting things accomplished. It makes little if any sense to blame those who created a system that supported and worked for the workplace needs of the time period. However, as the landscape of America changed—along with its workforce pools and composition— organizations fell woefully behind. Few organizations reflect the needs, backgrounds, and values of a diverse America and do not accommodate today's workforce in a way that effectively addresses its requirements for performance.

As far back as 1992, 52 percent of working adults were women, and 11 percent of the men were minorities, which means only 37 percent of working adults were white males—and the percentages of white males are decreasing. It just makes good business sense to reexamine a situation in which 63 percent of the workforce may be less productive than they could be because they work in an outdated system.

With ever-increasing amounts of change in the workforce, workplace diversity cannot be ignored. It is a critical challenge that must be faced. The first part of addressing the current trend of a multicultural, diverse workforce lies in knowing how diversity can impact your organization. It has both potential downsides and potential opportunities.

Potential Risks if Diversity Is Not Managed

Workplace diversity can impact an organization in many ways. If it is not managed properly, diversity can

❖ **Hinder productivity**. When diverse work teams are not trained to leverage the uniqueness they bring and fail to avoid barriers such as prejudice and stereotypes, productivity can suffer.

❖ **Create conflicts**. Generational conflicts between younger and more senior workers can occur.

❖ **Lead to communication gaps**. Words, phrases, and behavior have different contextual meanings in different cultures, which can lead to misunderstandings and failure.

❖ **Result in unfair hiring/promotional preferences**. During selection, interviewing practices of hiring to individual preferences versus real job requirements can develop. Candidates who are qualified based on the real job requirements might be overlooked, dismissed, or not even selected for an interview if these practices are not challenged.

Other workplace changes such as flattened organizations, the need for faster cycle times, and team-based or matrix organizational structures can prove challenging to those with an "old-school" model of how organizations used to work in the "homogeneous past." It can also be daunting to new entrants to the workforce who are not prepared to handle this new way of operating, especially if they are put in charge of a group who was accustomed to the old way.

There are some potential obstacles that must be overcome if an organization is to be successful. Some of them include the following:

❖ **Societal Traditions**. Certain occupations are sometimes associated with certain types of people. For example, in many societies, nurturing roles of secretary, nurse, social workers, and the like are primarily filled by women. Older workers and women are often excluded from physical jobs. Those who are physically or mentally challenged have difficulty finding work. Those who "buck the system" and obtain jobs in fields that have traditionally been held by people of the opposite sex typically encounter resistance.

❖ **Industry Norms**. Certain industries have norms that make it difficult for diverse individuals. For example, those in construction-related fields or the automotive industry often attend trade shows and conferences that are male dominated and include seductively dressed female spokesmodels. Women or individuals from different ethnic groups might feel uncomfortable being in those environments.

❖ **Lack of Awareness**. Many people might not be aware or "down play" the impact of diversity on a work environment.

They might not realize the impact on productivity, morale, competitiveness, etc. Only after their awareness has been raised can an organization be fully capable of achieving top-level performance.

❖ **Stereotyping**. Everyone stereotypes. Stereotypes are defined as fixed, inflexible notions about a group. Stereotypes, whether positive or negative, are the heart of prejudice, and they block the ability to think about people as individuals. Many stereotypical generalizations are based on misconceptions and errors in judgment. Sometimes people generalize too much or stereotype simply because they do not have all the facts, have limited personal experience, or are using distorted information that itself is based on stereotypes. In order to take advantage of diversity's potential, individuals must first learn to identify the stereotypical perceptions they hold, and then work toward changing them.

Potential Opportunities if Diversity Is Managed Effectively

Workplace diversity can be a tremendous strength and a real "ace in the hand" of an organization that uses these workforce assets strategically. Capitalizing on workplace diversity can help an organization

❖ **Gain a competitive advantage**. Coming up with improved ways and perspectives for doing things faster, cheaper, and better that might be as unique as the diversity of the group can translate into a unique competitive advantage.

❖ **Enter new markets**. Customers from different demographic groups, backgrounds, and countries can be added to the organization's market.

❖ **Become more creative and innovative**. As stated earlier, more and different input can be generated if these sharing behaviors are cultivated and utilized.

❖ **Increase employee satisfaction**. When employees don't understand one another, they become frustrated easily. Capitalizing on workplace diversity means learning how to accept differences and working well with others. This helps increase morale and satisfaction.

Diversity History and Approaches

Diversity History

To understand diversity from a contemporary perspective, it is helpful to briefly review the history of diversity in the U.S. workplace over the past 30 years. Several governmental initiatives have been enacted with regard to diversity. They include initiatives such as:

Civil Rights Act

This act was created as an outgrowth of the human rights movement and was enacted in 1964. It was the beginning of a wave of social change that continues even today.

Affirmative Action

Shortly after the Civil Rights Act of 1964, Affirmative Action legislation was enacted. Its intent was to ensure that employers took positive steps to attract, promote, and retain women and minorities if they were underrepresented in the organization's workforce. This legislation was forced onto employers and came to be viewed as "quota-filling," which sometimes created animosity between groups. While Affirmative Action was not the final solution, it was a necessary step appropriate for the times America faced.

Equal Employment Opportunity

Next, Equal Employment Opportunity legislation was enacted to prohibit discrimination on the basis of race, color, religion, sex, national origin, age, disability, or veteran status. It has been updated to include discrimination based on sexual orientation. EEO attempted to provide applicants and employees with equitable treatment in an organization's human resources and management practices, including recruitment, hiring, training, compensation, and promotion. The Equal Employment Opportunity Commission (EEOC) is now responsible for monitoring and enforcing legislation regarding workplace diversity.

Sexual Harassment

This area became a focus of business in the 1980s and 1990s. As more women entered the workforce, incidents of sexual intimidation on the job increased. Research has shown that a large percentage of women report having experienced some sort of sexual harassment. With recent publicity in this area, the courts are making awards on an increasing number of claims.

Americans with Disabilities Act

The most recent human rights legislation was the passing of the Americans with Disabilities Act (ADA) in 1990, which applies to 53 million Americans. ADA requires employers to make "reasonable accommodations" in employing people with job-related limitations. The main impact is on selection and job descriptions in employment, and in modifying facilities for buildings and retail outlets. The law includes people with HIV and AIDS, as well as many older people.

Approaches to Diversity

Throughout the years, there have been a number of approaches to manage diversity. Here are a few examples:

The Golden Rule

This approach suggested that we "treat each other like we would like to be treated." However, the majority culture assumed that this meant treating people according to the traditional standards already established. This approach left no room to acknowledge individual differences. This leaves a lot to be desired and does not effectively meet the needs of a diverse workforce.

Right the Wrongs

This approach is often likened to Affirmative Action. It acknowledges that minorities and women have been effectively mistreated when it comes to fair representation in organizations. It often generated a white male backlash and charges of reverse discrimination since some white males and others felt this was nothing but quotas to hire unqualified people and a means to take their jobs away. Dr. Roosevelt Thomas, author of "Beyond Race and Gender," wrote in a 1990 *Harvard Business Review* article:

> "What managers fear from diversity is lowering of standards, a sense that 'anything goes.' Of course standards

43

must not suffer. In fact, competence counts more than ever. The goal is to manage diversity in such a way as to get from a diverse workforce the same productivity that we once got from a homogeneous workforce. The diversity I'm talking about is not only race, gender, creed, and ethnicity, but also age, background, education, function and personality differences. The objective is not to assimilate minorities and women into the dominant white male culture, but to create a dominant heterogeneous culture."

The "right the wrongs" approach created an "us versus them" mentality, which destroys teamwork and productivity, and negatively impacts people and the bottom line.

Valuing Differences

The "Valuing Differences" approach is inclusive. It acknowledges differences and recognizes that they exist, but the approach doesn't require that people are assimilated into the dominant culture. It incorporates much of the current thinking related to diversity that focuses on diversity as a business imperative and asset.

By using a "Valuing Differences" approach, diversity becomes equally valuable to traditional employees, because it gives them the freedom to break out of the stereotypes they have been forced to conform to. For diversity to work, organizations must make certain that diversity is viewed as an asset to be utilized to meet its strategic business objectives.

Figure 2-3. Diversity Statistics Quiz Answers

1. By the year 2020, what will be the estimated percentage of females in the workforce? **Answer:** 50% according to Judy, R. W. & D'Amico, C. (1997). Hudson Institute Workforce 2020 Report. Indianapolis, IN: The Hudson Institute.

2. Of the 8.7 million immigrants who arrived in the United States between 1980 and 1990, what percentage have college degrees? What percentage of U.S. natives have college degrees? **Answers:** 23.7%; 20.3% respectively according to Fililowski, D. (1993, February). Perspectives. *Personnel Journal.*

3. In the United States, what percentage of male executives under age 40 are fathers? What percentage of female executives under age 40 are mothers? **Answers:** 90%; 35% respectively according to Solomon, C. M. (1990, April). Careers under glass. *Personnel Journal*, p. 102.

4. What are the two most racially and ethnically diverse states in the United States? The two least? **Answers:** New Mexico and California; Maine and Vermont. New Mexico's diversity index is 60, which means there is a 60 percent chance that any two randomly selected New Mexicans are different either racially or ethnically. California's diversity index is 59. Maine's and Vermont's diversity indexes are 4. Source: Meyer, P. (1991, April 11). Diversity index developed from 1990 Census statistics. *USA Today*, p. 1A.

5. How many people indicated they were "multi-racial" in the 2000 Census? **Answer:** Nearly 7 million Americans took advantage of the first opportunity to check off more than one race on their 2000 Census forms. More than 40 percent of those who did so were younger than 18, proof that the American populace will be even more diverse in

decades to come. Some businesses see that as a signal to start broadening their messages now. Source: Retrieved April 19, 2002, www.Diversityinc.com

6. Women make up _____ percent of all shoppers in the United States; they spend _____ cents of every dollar. **Answers:** Women make up **73 percent** of all shoppers in the United States; they spend **80 cents** of every dollar according to www.Diversitycentral.com

7. By the year 2050, what percent of the total U.S. population will Asians, Hispanics, African Americans, and other non-white groups represent? **Answer:** 47 percent. Source: Wellner, A. S. & Weisul, K. (1992, December 21). A spicier stew for the melting pot. *Business Week*, p. 26.

8. What demographic group represents the fastest growing customer base in the United States? **Answer:** Hispanics. Trudy Suchan, a cartographer in the Census Bureau's Population Division who helped publish a new atlas, said she thought the atlas showed "a surprising reach of the Hispanic population. We tend to think of the Hispanic population as existing only in the West and the Southwest. But this picture shows a greater reach." Source: Retrieved August 10, 2001, www.Diversityinc.com

9. What are the top six frequently cited barriers to advancement listed by women in the workplace? **Answer:**

❖   Lack of mentoring opportunities

❖   Commitment to personal and family responsibilities

❖   Exclusion from informal networks of communication

❖   Lack of women role models

❖ Failure of senior leadership to assume accountability for women's advancement

❖ Stereotyping and preconceptions of women's roles and abilities

Source: *Catalyst Newsletter* (2001, July). www.catalystwomen.org

10. One out of _____ African-American households makes more than $50,000 per year. Answer: 1 out of 8 (13 percent)

References

Chang, R. (1996). *Capitalizing on workplace diversity.* Irvine, CA: Richard Chang & Associates.

Dupont, K. (1997). *Handling diversity in the workplace.* West Des Moines, IA: American Media Publishing.

Hubbard, E. E. (1999). *How to calculate diversity return on investment.* Petaluma, CA: Global Insights Publishers.

Hubbard, E. E. (2002). *Techniques for managing a diverse workforce.* Petaluma, CA: Global Insights Publishing.

Humphreys, J. M. (2002, 2nd quarter). The multi-cultural economy 2002: Minority buying power in the new century. *Georgia Business and Economic Conditions Journal*, Vol. 62, No. 2.

Loden, Marilyn (1996). *Implementing diversity.* Chicago, IL: Irwin.

O'Mara, J. (1994). *Diversity activities and training designs.* San Diego, CA: Pfeiffer & Company.

Orey, M. C. (1996). *Successful staffing in a diverse workplace: A practical guide to building an effective and diverse staff.* Irvine, CA: Richard Chang & Associates.

Rasmussen, T. (1996). *The ASTD trainer's sourcebook: Diversity*. New York: McGraw-Hill.

Wright, P.; Ferris, S. P.; Hiller, J. S.; & Kroll, M. (1995). Competitiveness through management of diversity: Effects on stock price valuation. *Academy of Management Journal*, Vol. 38, n1, pp. 272–287.

Web sites:
www.Diversityinc.com
www.DiversityCentral.com

Chapter 3
The Differences Between Equal Employment Opportunity, Affirmative Action, and Managing Diversity

Knowing the differences between Equal Employment Opportunity (EEO), Affirmative Action (AA), and managing diversity (MD) is often cited as a major step forward in understanding what diversity really is. For many people, these three concepts are synonymous, but there are a variety of examples that illustrate how they are very different. Some employees see these terms as nothing new—simply a repackaging of Affirmative Action.

Confusion of Terms

One of the reasons for the confusion in the terms is the way they are discussed in the media. Dr. Taylor Cox and Ruby Beale, for example, cite a *Business Week* article (1991, July 8, p. 65) that clearly illustrates the media's influence and genesis that cause some of the confusion:

> "Call it affirmative action. Or minority outreach. Or perhaps you prefer 'managing diversity,' the newest, politically well-scrubbed name for policies aimed at bringing minorities into the mainstream through preferential hiring and promotion."

The language featured in this article takes the term *managing diversity*, which is a more comprehensive term in that it includes all types of groups and organizational activities, and reduces it to only one dimension of difference (race) and only one organizational activity (Affirmative Action). The choice to use this language was made despite the wide range of available literature that would have revealed a much broader definition of the term used by experts in the field.

The *Business Week* article further reduces Affirmative Action—which is defined in the executive order that created it as "systematic steps to ensure that past discrimination is remedied and that further discrimination does not occur" (Werther & Davis, 1993, p. 105)—to two actions: preferential hiring and promotion of minorities. To make matters worse, if you explore the article further, it suggests that racial minorities really come down to one group: African Americans. Finally, the message that managing diversity is merely a new name for Affirmative Action is further reinforced in the *Business Week* article (1991, July 8, p. 58) with the following statement: "To get past the emotional charge carried by Affirmative Action, some employers have embraced a new catch-phrase: managing diversity."

This type of confusion sets up a never-ending spiral of misunderstandings and barriers to effectively managing diversity. If diversity is defined as a new version of Affirmative Action, then all of the conceptual and motivational challenges that have plagued Affirmative Action will be attached to the process of managing diversity. They help fuel personal self-interest and a belief in maintaining the status quo theory that everyone has the opportunity to succeed. That personal—not situational— attribute determines a person's economic success or failure. In addition, the notion of self-interest refers to the fact that people will tend to resist actions or policies that they perceive will reduce their personal circumstances and support those that maintain or enhance them. When people believe that the organization's environment and systems are on their own fair, there is no wonder they believe the incorrect notion that managing diversity is the same as Affirmative Action. This failed understanding of the differences between these terms creates a whole host of problems and barriers to change in organizations.

Understanding the Differences

When organizations clearly understand the differences, they move beyond Affirmative Action–based profile improvement efforts that are focused solely on race and gender. They proceed to focus on the organizational environment and the degree to which the diversity of all groups is fully utilized, and organizational activities and systems are adjusted to build a more inclusive process directed toward performance. The goal is no longer merely satisfying legal requirements; instead, it now appropriately expands to include correcting environmental issues, improving productivity, and enhancing employee morale.

By focusing on the quality of the work environment and full utilization of diverse workforce talents to improve organizational performance, managing diversity takes a giant step beyond Affirmative Action. Its messages of respect, inclusion, and performance can help defuse the residue of confusion, resentment, and backlash that occurs in many organizations. These concerns are made worse by the sluggish U.S. economy, massive corporate downsizing, immigration concerns over the events of the September 11th terrorist attacks (where stereotypes of specific groups of people and their beliefs were challenged), the politics of division, and in some cases, poorly executed Affirmative Action programs. Managing the effects of these events and beliefs on organizational health and performance becomes critical.

Profile improvement will always be important and a requirement to build an effective organizational environment. As a
step in a larger process of managing diversity, it can now be
seen as a means to develop the path toward opportunities such
as innovation, opening new multicultural markets, effective
teamwork, and the like. As a new management paradigm, managing diversity holds the organization accountable for creating
a culture in which diversity thrives and is utilized to meet
bottom-line performance objectives.

While it is easy to see how the goals of Equal Employment
Opportunity, Affirmative Action, and diversity overlap, it is
important to recognize how they are different. Figure 3-1
describes some of the key differences.

Figure 3-1. Differences between EEO/AA and MD

EEO/Affirmative Action	Managing Diversity
Quantitative: Focuses on demo-graphic profile changes	**Quantitative and Qualitative:** Focuses on environmental readiness and performance improvement
Government Mandated: Imposed and often not welcomed	**Voluntary:** Internally driven and welcomed when properly explained and understood
Remedial: Focused on changing historic patterns of discrimination	**Strategic:** Focused on increas-ing innovation and creating a competitive advantage
Reactive: Problem response	**Proactive:** Opportunity-driven

(continued)

Figure 3-1. Differences between EEO/AA and MD *(concluded)*

EEO/Affirmative Action	Managing Diversity
Beneficiaries: Protected groups	**Beneficiaries:** Everyone
Initial Step	**Follow-up Step**
Culture Change: Not required	**Culture Change:** Required
Implementation: Compliance focused	**Implementation:** Competency, performance, and accountability focused

In many respects, managing diversity is an outgrowth of the early EEO and AA efforts to end discrimination, thus ending exclusionary behavior in organizations. It is a follow-up step that many organizations initiate after some internal profile changes have already occurred. Instead of ignoring cultural differences, managing diversity efforts encourage all members of the organization to increase their knowledge about diverse cultures to assist the organization in meeting its objectives. In addition to managing diversity, valuing diversity initiatives focus on bridging gaps and understanding among different cultural groups in an effort to create an inclusive workplace environment.

While the objectives of EEO, AA, and managing diversity are complementary, they can wind up on a collision course if the purpose of each is not made clear within the organization.

Workplace Diversity Self-Assessment

Developing a comprehensive implementation plan to institutionalize diversity requires that managers as change agents must question their own assumptions and understandings about workplace diversity and what it will take to get there. It requires commitment and accountability to the changing realities of a global marketplace, a willingness to address them, and an ability to integrate the organization's vision of future performance through the use of all diverse assets of the organization. Complete Exercise 3-1 to explore your own values, perceptions, and expectations about diversity.

Exercise 3-1. Self-Assessment

Examine how your values, perceptions, and expectations about diversity relate to your own behavior when you encounter people you manage who are different from yourself. Think back on your experiences over the last week and all of the individuals you encountered who were different. Or, in the week to come, complete this assessment based on your experience. Write your responses to the following six questions:

1. What was your first response or impression of this person when you first met them?

   _____

   _____

   _____

2. Examine the specific assumptions you made about the other person.

   _____

   _____

3. Check the reality behind your assumptions. (Were they stereotypes, prejudice, etc.?)

_____

_____

4. Identify what you plan to do differently about how you manage these responses.

_____

_____

5. Find commonalities and appreciate the differences between you.

_____

_____

6. Develop ways to build trust.

_____

_____

References

Cox Jr., T., & Beale, R. L. (1997). *Developing competency to manage diversity.* San Francisco, CA: Berrett-Koehler Publishers.

Crockett, R. O. (1991, July 8). Race in the workplace. *Business Week,* pp. 58, 65.

Dupont, K. (1997). *Handling diversity in the workplace.* West Des Moines, IA: American Media Publishing.

Loden, M. (1996). *Implementing diversity.* Chicago: Irwin.

Werther, W. B., & Davis, K. (1993). *Human resources and personnel management.* New York: McGraw-Hill.

Chapter 4
Barriers to Diversity

People are diverse in many ways. We have a number of differences that offer a wide range of opportunities and possibilities to make organizations successful and our world a better place. When we accept our differences and learn to work with them, we enrich our lives and improve the creativity and productivity of the organization. However, too often organizations find they work against the effective use of differences and allow them to hinder instead of help.

Why do we have so many problems dealing with diversity? Diversity itself isn't a problem—our differences have always been there; they are what make us unique. The problems lie in our attitudes toward diversity. People who have negative attitudes toward other people's differences often engage in negative behaviors including

❖ Prejudice

❖ Stereotyping and discrimination

❖ Ethnocentrism

To keep these negative behaviors from becoming barriers to organizational diversity, we must learn to recognize and avoid them in all types of situations such as working with employees, business relationships, customer relationships, hiring, firing, and the like. Prejudice, stereotyping, and discrimination hurt people and ultimately destroy an organization's effectiveness and bottom line. Let's explore these barriers in more detail.

Prejudice

Prejudice is a preconceived feeling or bias. Each of us has biases of one kind or another. Some people wouldn't be caught dead driving a certain make of car or wearing a certain brand of clothes. Other people may swear by that car or brand. We all have likes and dislikes. As long as our biases are about unimportant things, like our brand of toothpaste, they are relatively harmless. However, when we hold prejudices against other people, we create all kinds of problems.

Prejudice against people comes from a belief in the superiority of one's own race, culture, class, or other group. Often, prejudice takes this ethnocentric form. Although America was founded on the principle of "liberty and justice for all" and most people want to believe in equal rights, current studies show that 10 to 20 percent of Americans still express bigotry. However, there is a trend toward not openly expressing prejudice, but subliminally still viewing nontraditional employees as less competent (Dovido, 1993, p. 37).

Other studies highlight the impact of prejudice even further and show that even people who want to avoid bias are *conditioned* for a biased response. In one experiment, executives were given resumes and photos of job applicants and asked to describe jobs they might offer the people. All the resumes were identical, but the pictures were different: a white man, an African American man, a Hispanic man, an African American woman, and a Hispanic woman. White executives typically assigned administrative tasks to the women of color and line tasks to the men of color. Further, in an illustration of how broad reaching prejudices can be and how they can create internalized oppression, when women of color were given the same assignment with the

58

same photos and resumes as the white executives, they made the same job assignments.

Another study revealed that biased behavior is largely uncon-scious. People who display negative non-verbal reactions to others are usually unaware they are doing so (Bass, 1990). One of the most devastating aspects of prejudice is that people deny they have biases. Denying it only perpetuates the prob-lem. It can also be related to a sense of not wanting to admit to a loss of control, similar to incidents when people get lost and need directions. Often, they do not want to admit that they are lost and certainly don't want to admit it to a stranger!

At other times, prejudice can come in the form of "backlash" when people perceive diversity as nothing but an attempt to fill quotas and take jobs away from others. When this mind-set exists, resentment, poor teamwork, and sabotage can result that affects productivity. Some prejudice is a matter of blind conformity to prevailing cultural beliefs and customs. However, in most cases, prejudice seems to fulfill a specific irrational function for people such as making them feel supe-rior to others, or using others as scapegoats for the preju-diced person's own resentment or guilt. Prejudice is usually tied to a person's deepest fears, although the connection is normally subconscious and therefore hidden from awareness. Researchers have uncovered some interesting facts about prejudice:

❖ Prejudice is found in all types of people in every ethnic group.

❖ Prejudice occurs in the mind, but can be acted out in ways that exclude others.

❖ Prejudiced acts can be performed by non-prejudiced as well as prejudiced people.

❖ The best way to decide if an action is prejudiced is to notice how it affects another person. You can't prove someone is prejudiced, but you might prove that his or her actions excluded and placed another person at a disadvantage.

We talk about prejudice in terms of workplace prejudice, sexism, racism, ethnic prejudice, and other "isms." Workplace prejudice is active in organizational workplaces today. According to the National Opinion Research Center, some people still believe the stereotypes that women and ethnic minorities are less intelligent, less hard-working, less likely to be self supporting, more violence-prone, and less patriotic than they are. Organizations such as the U.S. Glass Ceiling Commission and Catalyst have stated in their research reports that prejudice is the biggest barrier to advancement that diverse employees face.

Sexism

Sexism is prejudice based on gender and is said by some to be the root of all prejudice and discrimination. As children we literally begin learning this form of inequality in the cradle. It doesn't involve a majority and minority, since men and women are relatively equal in number. However, women in all countries are a minority in economic and political arenas and have fewer rights and privileges than men.

Racism

Racism is typically a problem in societies such as the United States where there is a predominant majority group and one or more cultural minorities. People often use the term *racism* in discussions of prejudice. The term *race* has little meaning in anthropology. Because of intermarriages, you can have some experts say there are 3 races and others say there are 300. This fact notwithstanding, a major explanation for discrimination in society takes place in the name of race.

Ethnic Prejudice

People who try to distinguish between race and ethnicity typically say that racial traits are inborn, inherited, and given by nature, while ethnic traits are learned, cultural, and acquired through nurture. Since most ethnic characteristics are learned and are not permanently fixed in our genes, they can theoretically be changed. Ethnicity is much more flexible and changeable than race.

An ethnic subculture is a segment of a larger culture or society. Members of the subculture participate in shared activities in which the common origin and culture are significant ingredients. A subculture is unique because of its particular beliefs, customs and values, its heroes and heroines, its myths and stories, and its social networks. Ethnic discrimination against minorities occurs when "minority" status carries with it the exclusion from full participation in the society and the largest subculture holds an undue share of power, influence, and wealth.

Other "Isms"

Other isms include ageism, classism (or class snobbery), and homophobia (or antigay prejudice). Besides ethnic minorities and women, groups that experience discrimination in the workplace include persons with disabilities, gay people, older employees, and obese people. To a lesser extent, people from lower socioeconomic groups may be targets of prejudice, as symbolized by such derogatory terms as "trailer trash" and "poor White trash." Prejudice knows no boundaries, however, and some people believe that all Post Office employees are

deadbeat bureaucrats, all administrators are corrupt political
sharks, and so on. Complete Exercise 4-1 to examine your
experiences of being tolerated versus appreciated.

Exercise 4-1. Self-Assessment: Being Tolerated Versus Being Appreciated

Purpose: To experience the difference between tolerance and
appreciation.

Step One: Being Tolerated

❖ Think of a time when you felt tolerated. Write a few words
about it.

_____

_____

❖ How did it feel to be merely tolerated? Write a few words
about your feelings.

_____

_____

❖ How did feeling tolerated affect your relationship with the
tolerant person(s)?

_____

_____

❖ If it was a job situation, how motivated and effective were
you after you realized you were being tolerated?

_____

_____

Step Two: Being Appreciated

❖ Think of a time when you felt appreciated. Write a few words about it.

_____

_____

❖ How did it feel to be truly appreciated? Did you feel respected? Write a few words about your feelings.

_____

_____

❖ How did feeling appreciated affect your relationship with the appreciative person(s)?

_____

_____

❖ If it was a job situation, how motivated and effective were you after you realized you were truly appreciated?

_____

_____

❖ Based on this exercise, what are the lessons learned and/or what would you change in your own behavior from this point forward?

_____

_____

Stereotyping and Discrimination

As we discussed earlier, stereotypes are defined as fixed, inflexible notions about a group. Stereotyping occurs when we apply our biases to all members of a group. If you were raised to think all members of a particular ethnic group are lazy, you may still hold this stereotype, no matter what your day-to-day experience tells you. If you believe strongly in this stereotype, you may also spread it to others. A more technical look at stereotyping finds that it is a process that allows us to manage complex realities using categories to store information, to quickly identify things, to handle multi-sensory experiences, and to make sense of things. We often attach strong emotions to these stereotypes, even when they're false, and often use stereotypes to justify our dislike of someone.

We stereotype when we apply an experience with one member of a group to the entire group. If you met one member of a particular culture who was rude to you, it might be hard for you to recognize that not everyone from that particular group behaves in a rude way. But just because one member of a race, gender, age group, or culture acts a certain way, doesn't mean every other person of that group will act the same way. Your perceptions could be based on a lack of knowledge because you haven't taken the time to understand the other person's culture. Many stereotypical generalizations are based on mis-conception and errors in judgment.

Sometimes people generalize too much or stereotype simply because they do not have the facts, have limited personal experience, or are working with distorted information. Stereotypes often lead to assumptions that are insupportable and offensive. They cloud the fact that all attributes may be found in all groups and individuals. Stereotypes show up in phrases like "men won't ask for directions" or "you know 'those people' can't handle responsibility at this level." The stereotypes we attach to people hurt us as much as they hurt everybody else, because we can't get to know other people for who they really are. However, we can change when we discover how this stereotyping behavior develops.

We must deal with a lot of complexity in our lives and often need a process for sorting things out. When we stereotype, we form large classes or clusters of information for guiding our daily adjustments to life. We may not feel that we have time to get to know everyone and every situation, so for sanity's sake, we "generalize, delete, and distort" information to align it with information in broad categories. Unfortunately, we may associate this information with established categories just to make sense of the world. By doing so, however, it can prevent us from being completely open-minded.

These categories become our short cuts. We tend to place as much as we can in these classes or clusters to categorize events in order to take action. We are "inference focus beings" who like to solve problems. When left with little or no data, we will generalize, delete, and distort to come up with an answer to solve a problem or make sense of a person or situation. Because we like to problem solve as easily as possible, we try to fit things neatly into a category and use this category to judge what it is or means.

A stereotype enables us to readily identify related things. Stereotypes have a close and immediate tie with what we see, how we judge, and what actions we take. In fact, the purpose of stereotypes is to help us make responses and adjustments to life in a speedy, smooth, and consistent manner. For each mental category we create, we have a thinking and feeling tone or flavor. Everything in that category takes on that flavor. For example, we not only know what the term *Southern belle* means, we also have a feeling tone that is favorable or unfavorable that immediately comes to mind along with this concept. When we meet someone who we decide is a Southern belle, that feeling tone determines whether we like her more or less than we would if we got to know her on her own merits. Does labeling her as a "Southern belle" cause you to instantly predict that this experience will be pleasurable or painful?

Rationality and Justifying Our Fear

Stereotypes may be more or less rational. A rational stereotype starts to grow from a kernel of truth and enlarges and solidifies with each new relevant experience. A rational stereotype gives us information that we think can help us predict how someone will behave or what might happen in a situation. An irrational stereotype is one we've formed without adequate evidence. When you add emotions to this mixture, you get an overwhelmingly powerful sense of conviction about something that may or may not be based in truth. An irrational idea that is engulfed by an overpowering emotion is more likely to conform to the emotion than to objective evidence. Therefore, once we develop an irrational stereotype that we feel strongly about, it is difficult for us to change that stereotype based on facts alone. We must deal with the emotion and its ties to our deepest fears.

Sometimes we form stereotypes that are linked to an emotion related to fear such as hostility, suspicion, dislike, or disgust and set up the framework for prejudice toward an entire group of people based on our experience with one person or a few people. When people become prejudiced toward a group, they need to justify their dislike, and any justification that fits the immediate conversational situation will do. We constantly make others prove us wrong in our negative assumptions, rather than assuming the best. In addition, when people don't fit the stereotype, we think they're the exception rather than questioning our stereotype of them or the group they belong to.

Stereotyping is a double-edged sword. On one hand, it allows you to handle a world full of multi-sensory data so that you do not become overwhelmed; however, left on its own without a conscious understanding of how it affects the way we categorize, it can be fatally problematic. When our categorizations become too fixed, our labels too permanent, and our perceptions too rigid, it often leads to prejudice and discrimination against people.

Discrimination

Discrimination does not mean failing to hire enough women, minorities, or gays; it doesn't even mean refusing to associate with people from other cultures. Discrimination is treating people differently, unequally, and usually negatively because they are members of a particular group. We develop prejudices, turn them into stereotypes, and allow them to grow into discrimination. Unfortunately, prejudice, stereotyping, and discrimination are still facts of organizational life and our society with all the associated negative consequences. We see these diversity barriers in the form of racist or sexist jokes, rude remarks, or the refusal to hire or promote. If you encountered a person being discriminated against today, how would you handle it? Keep in mind doing nothing is taking a position. Complete Exercise 4-2 to gain some insight into this matter.

Exercise 4-2. What's Your Experience with Discrimination?

Have you ever been discriminated against? Have you ever witnessed someone being discriminated against? If so, what did you do? _____

_____

My Experience: _____

_____

_____

_____

_____

Situations I witnessed. What I did. _____

_____

_____

_____

_____

If others you know are discriminatory and you accept that part of them without protest, you are actually allowing discrimination to continue. You can discriminate by merely being a part of an organization that itself unintentionally discriminates through its traditional business practices. This can come about due to a power-privilege imbalance that automatically favors a dominant majority and is unfavorable to minorities—unfavorable, that is, until some actions are taken to offset and correct this imbalance. The press is filled with cases that highlight organizational inability to deal effectively with diversity and the financial and other costs incurred:

❖ Racial bias claims alone cost the U.S. economy about $215 billion a year. That's almost 4 percent of the gross domestic product (GDP).

❖ More than one-third of Fortune 500 companies have been sued for sexual harassment, many of them more than once. A *Working Women* magazine survey of Fortune 500 businesses as far back as 1988 determined that the direct costs of sexual harassment averaged $6.7 million annually per company in lost productivity, absenteeism, and turnover. One expert estimates that when overall gender bias is figured in, organizations lose over $15 million per year.

❖ Age discrimination cases are up since the Age Discrimination in Employment Act went into effect in 1967, with a median of $219,000 awarded in successful suits.

❖ Disability claims have also been rising since the Americans with Disabilities Act went into effect in 1990. It is having a major effect on the way organizations do business by adjusting access to include all available talent.

❖ Court costs, attorney fees, settlements, stress-related illnesses due to hostile work environment, poor productivity, poor quality, impacts on short-term and long-term disability insurance expenses, impact on customer service level maintenance, and ability to compete must also be included in the cost side of the ledger.

A power imbalance is a key aspect of discrimination. Power is a force that is absolutely essential to perpetuate discrimination. For example, an African American clerk may dislike a white executive and never try to get to know him as a person. Her actions are not called "discrimination" because she does not have the power to take actions that exclude him in ways that disadvantage his career. On the other hand, the executive does have the power to discriminate against her, and that type of power differential is not unusual. White men still hold nearly all of the top-level economic and political power in the United States. They hold 92 percent of the top-level positions in mid- to large-sized businesses and about 80 percent of the seats in Congress, even though they comprise only approximately 35 percent of the population and 39 percent of the workforce, according to the U.S. Census Bureau and the U.S. Glass Ceiling Commission. Civil rights measures are based on the fact that a power imbalance exists and represent an attempt to break the cycle of centuries of discrimination.

Discrimination against diverse workforce employees not only affects their career progress, it also affects their trust, motivation, and productivity in addition to their relationships with the rest of the workforce. It affects them in every phase and aspect of their work experience. These include areas such as

❖ **Recruitment Practices.** Examples include unwillingness to hire people who are different, selective advertising of high-level positions in media rarely used by minorities, etc.

❖ **Screening Practices.** Examples include using preferences as if they are real requirements to be effective in the job, stereotyping intelligence attributes to different groups, prejudices against education received at specific minority-focused colleges or universities, vague or arbitrary assessments made by others who may be prejudiced in their view then using that assessment to determine who will be interviewed.

❖ **Terms and Conditions of Employment.** Examples include the fact that women and minorities typically earn about 70 percent of the amount white males do for the same job with equivalent experience, and may receive fewer benefits and fewer opportunities to be in succession plans and development or mentoring experiences.

❖ **Tracking and Job Segregation.** Examples include "women jobs," "men jobs," and "minority jobs," even though in today's "politically correct" environment they would never be called that.

❖ **Performance Evaluation.** Examples include the way job performance of women and minorities is viewed versus others. Successful performance by women and African American men on tasks traditionally done by white males tends to be attributed to luck, while white men's performance is more likely attributed to their abilities according to the research of J. H. Greenhaus and S. Parasuraman (1991). Minorities and women are often held to a more limited range of acceptable behavior than others. Assertive behavior for example may be viewed negatively if exhibited by a woman or a person of color.

❖ **Promotion Practices.** Examples include unwritten, informal rules or expectations that are rarely shared and administered equally for women and minorities, prejudging a woman's career potential based on her family status.

❖ **Glass Ceilings, Sticky Floors, and Compressed Walls.** Examples include research that shows white men at the top of organizations prefer colleagues of their same gender and race and clear statistical evidence that shows multi-year patterns of poor development, succession planning, promotion, and retention of high-level minority and women executives.

❖ **Diverse Standards.** Examples include standards such as "not aggressive enough," "lacks initiative," "too passive," or "too emotional" when the real reason is misreading a person's cultural traits.

❖ **Layoff, Discharge, and Seniority Practices.** Examples include protecting workers who have been employed the longest, knowing that minorities and women are often the last hired and the first fired or laid off, or cannot get into the trades and other programs to meet seniority requirements. In some cases, minorities have been barred from certain occupations.

❖ **Career Alternatives.** Discrimination can make it even more difficult for diverse employees to choose alternatives to corporate careers that hit a glass ceiling. Many women and minorities, in general, may have fewer assets and more difficulty in getting business loans than do white men, however, this is changing. Use Exercise 4-3 as a tool to determine the privileges you may or may not have.

Exercise 4-3. Self-Assessment: How Privileged Are You?

Please respond to the following questions:

1. What are some privileges you enjoy in life? List a few.

   _____

   _____

2. How do privileges affect your life? Do they affect your
   personal power? Your ability to achieve your goals? Your
   success?

   _____

   _____

3. Which of these (or other) privileges are unavailable to some
   people because of the group they belong to? Beside each
   unavailable privilege, write the name of the group(s) that
   don't enjoy these privileges.

Privileges unavailable to others	Group(s) that don't enjoy this privilege

4. What are some privileges that are unavailable to you that people from certain groups enjoy? List each privilege and beside it, the group or groups that have access to it.

Privileges unavailable to me	Group(s) that have access to this privilege

5. How does this lack of privilege affect your life? Your personal power? Your ability to achieve your goals? Your success? _____

_____

Ethnocentrism

Another barrier to diversity that shows up in the workplace is "ethnocentric" behavior. Ethnocentrism is the belief that a person's own group is inherently superior to all others. People who exhibit ethnocentric behavior have a "my way or the highway" attitude that negates anyone else's opinion as worth considering.

Ethnocentrism, like prejudice, stereotypes, and discrimination, places barriers in the way of performance for those considered in the "out group." In order to be effective, ethnocentrism must be rooted out of the organization. It is counterproductive to high performance and dampens efforts of creativity and innovation.

Non-Verbal Communication

Our non-verbal communication or body language can be another obstacle to a diverse, high-performance work environment. Our actions do in fact speak louder than our words. When people know us as individuals, our gestures, eye contact, and odd movements are usually understood and, therefore, are not interpreted as threatening or negative. However, someone from another race, gender, culture, age, or economic background might easily misinterpret them. Although our world is becoming smaller, there isn't a common language, culture, or set of mannerisms. No gestures are universal. Worse yet, sometimes our tongues say one thing, our gestures say another thing, and our symbols (clothing, jewelry, hairstyles, facial hair, body markings) say still another thing. Mixed signals can be very misleading to other people, especially people who come from an area where the words, gestures, or symbols mean something entirely different.

Gestures

Have you ever folded your arms, flashed a victory sign, extended your left hand to someone as a handshake, made direct eye contact with someone while talking, etc.? If you have, you have offended someone in a particular culture. For example, the victory sign shown with the palm inward is an insult with vulgar overtones to Australians. It's easy to offend someone without even knowing it.

The gestures that mean "OK" to people born and raised in the United States have various meanings in other countries. To a co-worker from Japan, for example, it means "money." To business associates who grew up in France, Belgium, and Tunisia, it signals "worthless" or "zero." To those from Turkey, Greece, and Malta, it refers to homosexuality. To people who grew up in the rest of Europe and Mexico, this gesture represents an obscene or lewd comment. The crooked finger that native-born Americans use to say "Come here" is also considered obscene in many cultures. It's often the way people call prostitutes, animals, or "inferior" people! So it is easy to see that you could insult someone from another culture without even knowing it or why it might have been offensive.

Movement

Something as simple as how we sit and the position of our body can communicate a negative message. For example, people with a European heritage are sometimes offended by the way American men cross their legs while sitting. From their perspective, it is considered crude. Americans on the other hand may consider some European men effeminate due to the way they cross their legs and the lack of firmness in their handshake.

Even when you talk with Americans, there are different messages communicated by the way people in America sit, stand, shake hands, or cross their legs. There is plenty of room for things to be misunderstood. A woman with her arms crossed around her chest may not signal that she is closed to anything you have to say—she could be cold or it could simply be the way she likes to stand. A person with a weak handshake may have arthritis or some other malady that affects the strength of their handshake.

Personal Space

People often have their own comfort zones with distances from themselves. Have you ever watched what happens to a person's level of comfort when they are in a crowded elevator? Ever notice how close or far away people stand to senior executives if they are first-level employees? Have you ever approached someone and had him/her back away from you? It might be that people from this person's culture don't like having people close to them whereas you might have been raised to stand close to someone. Here are some comfort zone distances that have been found to be true among certain cultures:

❖ Native-born Americans—8 inches to 3 feet

❖ Mexican Americans—closeness up to 18 inches

❖ Japanese Americans—3 to 6 feet

Often, people may not consciously set these social distances, however, they just know that when others come close, they feel uncomfortable. Nonetheless, personal space is always based on the needs of the other person. You should pay close attention to how another person responds in words, tone and inflection, and body language. If that person winces, backs up, looks confused or worried, etc., be honest: Ask if there is anything you are doing that is making them uncomfortable.

Eye Contact and Touching

Eye contact follows the same rules as personal space. In American culture, it is not unusual for people to maintain eye contact for extended periods of time. It reflects a sense of power and confidence. In many cultures, however (especially those of Asian, Mexican, Latin American, Native American, and Caribbean), less eye contact is more respectful. Many African Americans were also raised this way. When some managers do not get a direct gaze from their employees, customers, or co-workers, they view these individuals as less confident and perhaps timid. This might even get interpreted as if the person has done wrong or something they are guilty or ashamed of. Of course, jumping to these conclusions based on these observations leads to all kinds of misunderstandings and poor performance.

Touching is another sensitive area. Some managers feel that due to their position of authority, they can touch employees without causing people to be offended; however, they may become offended if a member of their support team touched them or stood too closely. The rules of equality say that we should not use a behavior without being willing to receive it as well, and, most importantly, it must not violate the rules of sexual harassment. Shaking hands is always a polite way to greet people in America, and occasionally, a pat on the back. In some other countries, touching is forbidden or discouraged. In many Asian countries, body contact is considered disrespectful; instead, a nod or bow is more appropriate.

Sense of Time

Many people and cultures have different sensitivities to time. The notion of "being on time" has a number of different meanings. In some countries, arriving at an appointment at exactly the agreed-upon time is considered late, especially if the expectation is that you should always arrive at least 10 minutes early. In other countries, arriving one-half hour after the appointed time is fine since time is viewed as relative. Many Mexican Americans consider themselves punctual up to 30 minutes past the scheduled time.

Punctuality is highly valued by business-oriented Americans. They rush to and from everything and place a high priority on meeting deadlines. To people from other cultures and upbringings, however, time may have less significance. Native Americans, for instance, believe that since you can't be in two places at once, you should be wherever you are needed when you are needed rather than be governed by the clock. This doesn't mean that they disregard time or schedules; it's just that they value the concept of time differently.

You might ask, how could anything get done if everyone has different ideas about time? In a business meeting, everyone should be slightly flexible, but should not be expected to wait very long. Accepted protocol says that 15 minutes is long enough to wait for an appointment in the United States. If you have somewhere else to go or do, leave a note explaining that you waited as long as you could and will reschedule as soon as possible.

It is important to understand each person's sensitivities and the impact on organizational performance. When you are able to understand and respect things from their cultural perspective, it will help you avoid some of the major interpersonal barriers to diversity. The costs of these interpersonal missteps go far beyond any financial expenses.

Accepting Differences

As long as we are all different, there will not be one standard of behavior that will be identical. What is appropriate for one person or one culture will not be appropriate for another. Our values, beliefs, and customs will highlight significant differences in communication that signal whether someone is perceived as being respected or not. The concept of "independence," for example, is emphasized in American culture, so people grow up with the value and belief that mobility is OK. Friendships may be fleeting and possibly short term. However, more traditional cultures emphasize family and long-term relationships. People who grew up in European, Asian, and other cultures don't move around quickly or easily. They are often born and die in the same city, town, or village. They tend to take time to get to know people for the long term. So, for example, if you are friendly at work, some people from more traditional cultures might not understand why you don't invite them to socialize outside of work.

When the workplace includes people with diverse standards, values, and beliefs for how relationships are formed, it can cause challenges, misunderstandings, and an unfriendly work environment. One person might appear pushy while another might seem formal and distant. How people socialize, what constitutes teamwork, and what serves as a reward or not will be dictated by our differences. To be effective in eliminating barriers and handling the challenges of managing in an increasingly multicultural and global society, you will need to be highly competent in the use of a wide range of communications skills. Exercise 4-4 helps identify and rank barriers to diversity in your organization.

Exercise 4-4. Self-Assessment: Identifying Organizational Barriers to Diversity

Instructions

Rank in order the barriers to diversity (listed on the following page) that you perceive in your organization. The most significant barrier ranks as "1" in the list and the least important as "10."

Interpreting Your Answers

As you review your answers to the prioritized list, ask yourself the following questions:

❖ Are there any barriers you would like to add that were not found on the list?

❖ What is the impact of the organization of not dealing with each of these barriers?

❖ Based on answers to the previous question, which three barriers are the most significant or costly?

❖ What do you see happening to morale and productivity if you do nothing?

❖ What needs to happen in order to tear down some of these barriers?

❖ Where is a good place to begin?

Rank	Barrier
	Fear of hiring less-qualified, under-skilled, uneducated employees
	Strong belief that the current system is already fair to everyone
	Culture where stereotypes and prejudice toward different groups (such as race, gender, ethnicity, sexual preferences, age, etc.) are significant
	Diversity is not seen as a strategic priority for the organization
	Reluctance to dismantle existing systems to integrate diversity
	Few diversity champions willing to take a leadership role
	Perception that there has been a lot of progress in diversity already
	Confusion over the difference between Managing Diversity, EEO, and Affirmative Action
	Cost of implementing a diversity effort
	Concerns of being sued if attention is brought to this issue

Adapted from Gardenswartz, L., & Rowe, A. (1994). *The managing diversity survival guide.* Boston: McGraw-Hill.

References

Bass, J. (1990). Bias below the surface. *The Washington Post*, p. A2.

Carr-Ruffino, N. (1999). *Diversity success strategies.* Boston: Butterworth Heinemann Publishers.

Dr. Dovido, J. (1993). *The subtlety of racism.* Report: One America in the 21st Century: Forging the Future. Washington D.C.: U.S. Printing Office.

Dupont, K. (1997). *Handling diversity in the workplace.* West Des Moines, IA: American Media Publishing.

Gardenswartz, L., & Rowe, A. (1994). *The managing diversity survival guide.* Boston: McGraw-Hill.

Greenhaus, J. H., & Parasuraman, S. (1991). *Job performance attributions and career advancement prospects: Organizational behavior and decision processes.* Orlando, FL: Academic Press.

Hubbard, E. E. (2002). *Techniques for managing a diverse workforce.* Petaluma, CA: Global Insights Publishing.

Kennedy, D. (2000). *Assessment: Defining current realities.* San Francisco, CA: Berrett-Koehler Communications.

Kennedy, D. (2000). *Achievement: Measuring progress; celebrating success.* San Francisco, CA: Berrett-Koehler Communications.

Morrison, A. (1992). *The new leaders' guidelines on leader-ship diversity in America.* San Francisco, CA: Jossey-Bass.

National Opinion Research Center (1990, December). *Ethnic images, GSS topical report no. 19.* Chicago: University of Chicago.

Rasmussen, T. (1996). *The ASTD trainer's sourcebook: Diversity.* New York: McGraw-Hill.

Chapter 5
Developing Competencies for Managing Diversity

Introduction

When it comes to managing diversity, many managers often ask, "When I'm managing a diverse work group, what should I do that is different than managing any other group?" This is certainly a legitimate question and deserves an answer. Managers often feel that performing the primary management tasks of planning, organizing, directing, and controlling should be more than enough preparation to handle any situation. It is certainly true that these skills and competencies will go a long way in assisting a manager to accomplish organizational work; however, managing diversity and creating inclusive, productive work groups require additional awareness, knowledge, and skills to be effective.

First they need awareness about their own comfort with differences as well as their assumptions about those differences.

Beyond awareness of their own subtle expectations, there is a need for knowledge about different cultural norms, lifestyle needs, and personal preferences of individuals from different groups. For example, a manager might wonder, "Why do some employees speak their native languages at work even when they know English?"

Finally, managers have skill needs in the area of management responsibilities such as giving feedback, reviewing perform-ance, and building productive work teams (Gardenswartz & Rowe, 1994). They need answers to skill-related situations and questions such as the following:

❖ **Situation:** A physician gives directions to a Filipino nurse. When he asks if she understands the procedure, she nods her head and says yes. Later, the physician notices her doing the procedure incorrectly. In exasperation he asks, "Why didn't you tell me if you didn't understand? How can I give directions to someone who won't tell me when he/she doesn't understand?"

❖ **Question:** How can I give a performance review that does not cause a decline in motivation because of hurt feelings?

❖ **Question:** How can I keep my staff from segregating into separate ethnic, racial, or gender groupings?

❖ **Question:** What training and development needs do I have regarding my needs for awareness, knowledge, and skills related to effectively managing diversity?

❖ **Situation:** A manager becomes angry because one of his Latino employees takes the day off each time his wife needs to go to a doctor's appointment. The manager can-not understand the need to do this, since he has been told in other situations that the employee's wife drives and takes care of shopping and other errands on her own.

Awareness

Complete Exercise 5-1 to reveal your perceptions.

Exercise 5-1. Reflections Exercise

Take a moment to picture in your mind each of the following individuals:

❖ A law enforcement officer

❖ A successful corporate executive

❖ A great artist

❖ A renowned heart surgeon

❖ A master burglar

❖ A secretary

❖ A welfare recipient

❖ A classics professor

❖ A migrant farm worker

❖ A nurse

❖ A drug dealer

❖ A computer whiz

What does each individual from Exercise 5-1 look like in your mind's eye? What was their race or ethnicity? What was their gender? How tall or short were they? How stout or skinny were they? What was the color of their hair? Did they wear glasses? Were their clothes crisp and neat or wrinkled and ragged? How old was each individual? Did they have any apparent physical disabilities? If you heard their voice, what would they sound like? What did you feel (any physical sensations, uneasy, angry, annoyed, comfortable, trusting, etc.) just thinking about a person with this label? If you are like most people, your visual images, auditory recollections, and emotional state might be fueled by various stereotypes, some of them based on race and gender. You are rare indeed if your nurse or secretary wasn't a woman, your classics professor a tweedy, white male, or your welfare recipient a portly African American or Hispanic woman.

The point here is that the instant perceptions we form of others—often before even a single word is spoken or a handshake takes place—often determine the course we will take as we interact with them. And if this is the case, this process has many implications for affecting fair and equitable treatment for all employees, especially women and minorities. It could affect a person's ability to see clearly and compassionately during a conversational exchange and affect the outcome of the conversation. It might affect how fully these individuals will be able to contribute to the bottom line—by providing ideas, suggestions, problem-solving approaches, and process changes—and make a business case for new products and services for non-traditional markets (Fernandez, 1999).

In other words, due to our cultural misperceptions and lack of awareness, judgments based on racist or sexist stereotypes will clearly inhibit successful interactions among managers, employees, customers, and others because they undercut trust and respect. We cannot build up trust and respect on the basis of incorrect or incomplete information about the people we are trying to interact with. It is not healthy for either party, and the consequences can be costly to the organization. The impact includes misunderstandings, resentment, low morale, poor productivity, lawsuits, rampant mistakes, customer dissatisfaction, and under-served markets.

Cultural Programming

When managing diversity, cultural programming often creates people who suffer from what is known as the "*No-Knows,*" that is, "the things they don't know they are supposed to know." For example, if you don't know that you are supposed to know how to recognize and respond to someone who won't tell you he/she doesn't understand, then how do you find out that you should have known that? Confusing? It can be, especially if you have been raised in an environment where the norm was "if someone didn't understand something, it is up to him or her to speak up and say so." The culture we grow up in represents "behavioral software" that programs our perceptions of what is "the normal or natural way of doing things." It creates the lenses we use to see the world and strongly influences the choices we make for the "right way to behave" in a particular situation.

All of us are programmed by cultural "software" that determines our behavior and attitudes, from our response when making eye contact with someone, to whom we choose to give a smile, to how we deal with conflict, or to the choice of words we use to describe someone. Cultural programming guides our behavior. Without this programming, we would be as useless as a computer without software. Our culturally programmed awareness teaches us how to interact with one another, how to solve life's daily problems, and, in effect, how to move through and control the world around us. No society exists without these rules, and no individual is culture-free.

Our culture is more than manners. It drives, directs, and selects the subtlest aspects of our behavior, such as how long to wait between sentences, when it is acceptable to interrupt someone, and how to interpret the look on someone's face. Though most cultural rules are never written, they are all the more powerful because they are absorbed unconsciously as we watch others and their reactions to us.

It is easy for us to accept and understand that while we may eat cereal and juice for breakfast, someone else is having tortillas, rice, grits, ham hocks, or black coffee and cigarettes. However, when it comes to interpreting each other's behavior, cultural differences make understanding more difficult. To make matters worse, when we interpret another person's behavior through our own "cultural perceptual filters" (our software), we make mistakes. We take the nodding head to mean, "I understand," rather than "Yes, I heard you," as in the case of the Filipino nurse. We think the quick smile means the person is friendly and affable, rather than thinking he or she might be uncomfortable and perhaps embarrassed by our behavior or his or her own confusion. Or we assume that the employee who does not speak out in staff meetings is not a go-getter, is not assertive, or worse yet is stupid, when in fact he or she might be showing you respect by internalizing his or her ideas.

How does this misinterpretation happen? Generally it happens through a lack of awareness, knowledge, and understanding. According to Adler and Kiggunder (1983), when we encounter another's behavior, we need to make sense of it, so we follow a three-step process. First, we describe what we see, as in the case of a Latino employee: "This employee has refused a promotion to a management position." Second, we interpret the behavior: "He is not interested in getting ahead and is

missing a wonderful opportunity." Third, we make an evaluation: "He lacks initiative, is ungrateful for this opportunity,
lacks confidence, or any combination of these."

Steps two and three are the ones that get us in trouble in our
intercultural interactions. A critical step in bridging the gap is
learning more about other cultures' programming so that we
can avoid making incorrect assumptions about someone's
behavior. For example, if you knew that the individual in the
previous scenario was a young Mexican immigrant, you would
consider that he might be avoiding the promotion because in
his culture, being a part of a group is more important than
advancement or because it would put him in a supervisory
position over his friends and/or an older man from his same
culture. Since by his norms, elders are respected and promotions are made by age, he would be very uncomfortable being
forced to embarrass himself and his older compatriot by giving
the older worker orders.

Our awareness is based in large part on the basic cultural
programming we received during our developmental years.
Therefore our software and lenses are a product of the values
and beliefs we learned from life-learning sources such as
home, church, school, state, peer-group, etc. This creates a
bias, mental leaning, or inclination to see things a particular
way. We become partial to lenses that reflect a certain point
of view. Over time, this point of view can harden into stereotypes or fixed notions and mental patterns that generate
assumptions about what we should consider "normal" and
"different."

If these stereotypes are left unchecked, they can develop into
prejudice—they take the form of a judgment or an opinion
formed before any real facts are known, usually as an

unfavorable preconceived idea that is held in spite of facts to the contrary. Worse still, this prejudice can lead to discrimination. Discrimination takes place when we make distinctions in treatment and show partiality in favor of or prejudice against someone or something. Ultimately, it can lead to racism and other "isms" such as sexism, classism, ageism, etc. At this level, our behavior can reflect programs (institutionalized) and practices of racial and other discrimination, segregation, persecution, and domination.

Therefore, the first stage in any learning process to develop competency for managing diversity is to become self-aware. This includes becoming aware of your own cultural programming and your own limitations. For example, to begin your own self-awareness journey, you might ask, "What are my unconscious expectations of African Americans? Latinos and Latinas? Women?" "Am I surprised when secretaries or nurses aren't women, or when I meet doctors or executives who are?" Complete Exercise 5-2 to help you understand your cultural programming.

Exercise 5-2. Self-Assessment: Understanding Your Cultural Programming and Others

Instructions: This is an exercise to identify the influences that might have played a role in your cultural programming and to strengthen your self- and general-awareness. It is broken into two parts. Part One (pages 94–95) asks you to reflect on the influences that played a role in your development over the years to the best of your knowledge. When responding to the "Next 5 Years" section, you are being asked to forecast what might be true for you during that period.

Part Two (page 96) asks you to reflect on your knowledge of generational influences. Based on the birth years across the top row, fill in as much information as you can that addresses the items listed. Begin by filling in responses for the period of your birth year. Then list what you know about the other years listed. A few ideas are listed as examples.

Part One: Your Developmental Influences

Identify the influences you have experienced during the following periods of your life:

Period	0–12 years old	13–20 years old	21–current	Next 5 Years
Important Values and Beliefs: ❖ List your top 3–5 values and beliefs that guided your life during this period ❖ Changes over time? ❖ Events driving the change? ❖ Diversity management implications?				

Who were your heroes?	Religious affiliation(s)	Income status: Low, middle, affluent	Neighborhood: 1. Homogeneous 2. Mixed (25% or more of other groups)	Close Friends: 1. Homogeneous 2. Mixed (25% or more of other groups)

Part Two: Generational Influences

List the information for the period of your birth year first, then add what you know about others.

Birth Years	1922–1943	1943–1960	1960–1980	1980–2003
Popular Names for this Generation	Veterans	Baby Boomers	Generation Xers	The Nexters or Generation Y
What was the music of their early years?	❖ Swing ❖ Big Band	❖ Rock 'n Roll ❖ Elvis	❖ Disco ❖ Michael Jackson	❖ Alternative Rap ❖ Backstreet Boys
What defining events and trends?	❖ The Great Depression	❖ Television	❖ Computers	❖ School Yard Violence
Which well-known people were born during this period?	❖ Phil Donahue ❖ Gloria Steinem	❖ Bill Clinton ❖ Oprah Winfrey	❖ Brad Pitt ❖ Michael Jordan	❖ Kerri Strug ❖ Tara Lipinski
Core Values	❖ Dedication/Sacrifice ❖ Conformity ❖ Law and Order	❖ Optimism ❖ Health and Wellness ❖ Team Orientation	❖ Diversity ❖ Techno-literacy ❖ Fun	❖ Confidence ❖ Street Smart ❖ Optimism

Adapted from Zemke, R., Raines, C., Filipczak, B. *Generations at work.*

Key Questions to Answer:

1. What impact did the influences you identified in Part One have on your level of awareness?

2. What impact did the influences you identified in Part Two have on your level of awareness?

3. Based on the information about each generation collected in Part Two, what challenges would these observations pose for managing diversity?

4. How might your own "cultural software programming" add benefits and present challenges for working with others who are different from you in your personal and work lives?

As you become more self-aware, you must become self-aware of what you don't know about the lenses others use to perceive the world and what is "normal and natural" to them. That requires knowledge and understanding.

Knowledge and Understanding

Knowledge and understanding are key areas that influence how we respond to workforce diversity, according to Mendez-Russell, co-author of the *Discovering Diversity Profile* (1994). Diversity knowledge is defined as "the extent to which an individual possesses information about others from diverse backgrounds and cultures." If developed properly, a person's knowledge base will proceed from notions of stereotypes due to cultural programming to a level of information. When a manager operates with rudimentary awareness from basic cultural programming, stereotypes can develop because there is limited data. With this limited data, managers tend to make generalizations about people. Many of these generalizations are based on stereotypes—they operate on fixed images of groups of people that influence the ways the manager relates to individuals who are a part of that group. Stereotypes may possess some elements of fact in them, but each exaggerates and goes beyond the reality of fact. These generalizations may become "frozen" in the manager's mind. Even though he or she receives evidence to the contrary, they continue to hold on to these images as if they were fact.

As you build your knowledge base, you can progress to a more informed level of information. At this stage in your development, by gathering factual data from books, magazines, videos, articles in the media, casual conversation, formal training, and other sources, your images and viewpoints receive "enhanced programming." The more accurate information we have about others, the more likely it is that we will develop appropriate opinions, feelings, and behaviors. As you gather more information, it is possible to move your knowledge to an even higher level called understanding.

Understanding can be defined as "the extent to which an individual comprehends how others feel and why they behave as they do." The basic level of understanding helps us see that our personal reality is not the only reality and apply our knowledge and information based on how it feels to interact with people who are different from ourselves. It clarifies who we are in comparison to other people's perceptions of us. This gives us a basis for contrasting our cultural software programming with someone who is different. It opens the door to the possibility that with our unique individual programming, two people can view the same situation differently, and that difference is OK.

As your understanding grows, you are able to reach a level of "empathy" where you are able to show your ability to make connections with others on an emotional level. Managers who are empathic and possess mature levels of understanding can comprehend the emotions others are experiencing. They tend to recognize the reasons for the other person's point of view based on their cultural programming. Empathy allows us to wear another person's glasses and put ourselves in their shoes, trying to perceive "how it feels to look at the world through their lenses and walk their way." It makes us more flexible and less resistant, allowing us to become more sensitive to the differences among ourselves.

If we work on our knowledge and understanding to build our diversity maturity and effectiveness curve, we will ultimately get to a level of acceptance—we begin to respect and value the diverse characteristics and behaviors of others. This level of respect goes beyond simply "putting up" with others' differences or "being tolerated." Remember your observations in Exercise 4-1, "Tolerated versus Appreciated"? Few people, if any, simply want to be tolerated.

When you are a respectful manager in the diversity sense, you are able to grant full regard to the other person without compromise, based totally on the qualities they bring to the task at hand. Your views of the other person are not blemished or tarnished by negative cultural or racial characterizations. When you truly show respect for someone who is different from yourself, you see the value in having people contribute based on their background and culture. In fact, you appreciate their differences as added value to the organization. When managers create an atmosphere of respect for diversity, it creates trust and, in many cases, helps stimulate improved productivity.

Behavioral Skills

As an effective diversity manager, at a behavioral level, you must be able to interact with others who are different from yourself. This requires that you

❖ Understand your values, motives, and personal beliefs and their effect on what you do behaviorally.

❖ Conduct your own personal development work to take inventory of your strengths, weaknesses, and level of sensitivity and to understand the impact you have on others through your actions.

❖ Maintain a level of accountability to develop the skills necessary to adjust your behavior while still maintaining your own identity, values, and beliefs.

Knowing who you are and how your actions impact others clarifies your choices to select the most appropriate behavior.

A very skillful, diversity sensitive manager can effectively manage situations and successfully interact with people who may be different from themselves. When operating at this level, you are able to modify your behavior to meet the needs of the situation. Being effective in diverse workforce situations by using interpersonal skills reflects an ability to be flexible in reacting to the ideas and opinions of others. It demonstrates respect and trust through cooperation, attentiveness, and friendliness. This helps create an inclusive, high-performing workplace that can make a significant difference in organizational performance.

A beginning list of "Skills for Managing Diverse People" was published in the *Cultural Diversity at Work* newsletter published by The GilDeane Group in Seattle, Washington.

The list was developed collaboratively with managers, readers, workshop participants, and the editors of the publication. This list can be used to help you answer the question, "What am I supposed to do differently?" and you will see areas in which you might need to add skills to your repertoire. It identifies the skills grouped into seven categories. These skills apply to a wide range of management functions, including coaching, counseling, facilitating, interviewing, and conducting perform-ance reviews. The following interpersonal skills are important in managing a diverse workforce:

Modify your listening skills:

❖ Recognize and adapt to the variety of listening behaviors you will encounter among diverse people.

❖ Listen for value-based cultural assumptions and expectations.

❖ Observe behavior and monitor your interpretations and meanings.

Ask necessary and appropriate questions:

❖ Learn about other views, work styles, assumptions, and needs. Encourage others to do the same.

❖ Be comfortable in asking questions about the proper or preferred terminology, pronunciations, etc.

❖ Be comfortable in asking if you have caused offense, and find out how to correct and avoid it.

❖ Ask people to explain such things as goals, objectives, instructions, and directions in order to ensure common understanding.

Shift frame of reference when necessary:

❖ Demonstrate an understanding that perceptions are relative, and help others understand this.

❖ Demonstrate empathy and understanding for other values, attitudes, and beliefs; distinguish empathy from acceptance.

❖ Be flexible in your approach to situations; there are many ways of doing things.

Manage conflict constructively:

❖ Define the issue(s) in the conflict and focus on interests, not positions.

❖ Make an effort to understand other's perspectives.

❖ Demonstrate an understanding of different cultural assumptions about what conflict is and alternative ways of dealing with it.

❖ Develop a collaborative ("win-win") problem-solving process.

Recognize stereotypes and generalizations:

❖ Be aware of and monitor your own stereotypes.

❖ Hold others accountable for their stereotypes.

❖ Learn to distinguish between individual differences and cultural differences.

Show respect and interest in the other person:

❖ Become acquainted with the geography, language, history, politics, and customs of the native countries and cultures of those around you.

❖ Be aware that humor is perceived and handled in different ways by different cultural groups; inappropriate humor may be perceived as insulting.

❖ When talking with non-fluent English speakers, speak clearly and avoid jargon and slang. Ensure that the person understands your meaning.

Be approachable:

❖ Let others know, verbally and non-verbally, that you are willing to interact with them.

❖ Give cultural information freely when it is requested.

❖ Be open and accommodating to others' needs for gaining information; do not assume they know what you know.

❖ Learn to feel and exhibit comfort with groups and individuals different from yourself.

Developing skills to effectively manage a diverse workforce is no longer optional. In fact, these skills were required some time ago as our workforce demographic makeup changed. To be effective, managers must move through the continuum of becoming self-aware, improving their knowledge and understanding of diversity and translating that awareness, knowledge, and understanding into a conscious decision to behave in a way that values the differences that employees bring to the workforce.

Setting the Tone for Valuing Diversity

Setting the tone for an environment that values diversity is a critical responsibility for any manager. Leading by example is the best method for letting employees know that you value diversity and encourage them to do so as well. Setting and living up to the behavioral standards for valuing diversity may not always be easy since our cultural programming can influence our basic response. However, if we let others know that we appreciate their differences and show that appreciation through our behavior and actions, workforce members begin to get the message that valuing diversity is truly a standard in which you believe and something they should do.

Even more importantly, as a manager, you must role model important decisions such as hiring, promotion, and allocating rewards in a way that is consistent with valuing diversity. Dr. R. Roosevelt Thomas (2001) described this familiar situation in a *Harvard Business Review* article:

> "When I asked a white male middle manager how promotions were handled in his company, he said, 'You need leadership capability, bottom-line results, the ability to work with people, and compassion.' Then he paused and smiled. 'That's what they say. But down the hall, there's a guy we call Captain Kickass. He's ruthless, mean-spirited, and he steps on people. That's the behavior they really value. Forget what they say.'"

If behavior that is the direct opposite of valuing diversity is allowed to go uncorrected or addressed, employees get the message pretty clearly that this diversity and valuing differences stuff is nothing but "lip service." Managers must assess their behavior often, ask for feedback, hold themselves accountable, and "walk the talk" if real change is to occur.

Some managers try to walk the talk by adhering to the Golden Rule, that is, "treating others as *you* would like to be treated." It sounds good in theory; however, this approach can unintentionally project your own cultural programming related to perceptions, values, and beliefs of what is right and wrong, good and bad, and appropriate and inappropriate onto others whose needs, values, and beliefs are dramatically different. For example, in some cultures it is considered impolite or down right rude to bring attention to yourself in a group meeting. Yet some managers might not know that by recognizing a work-team member in front of others could be embarrassing to them and to members of their culture who might be in attendance. The assumption that people want to be treated the way you would want to be treated leads to "one-size-fits-all thinking." It assumes that if you like it, others will like it too. Instead, it might be more effective to practice the Platinum Rule, that is, "treat others as *they* want to be treated." This approach values what is needed from the other person's perspectives, values, and beliefs.

To find out what others want, you can ask questions of them directly, such as:

1. What do you want most from your job?

2. Under what conditions do you do your best work?

3. How would you like me to show recognition for your hard work?

4. How would you like to receive suggestions for improving your work?

5. What are your short- and long-term career goals?

6. In what ways do you think people in our department, including yourself, are different from one another?

7. How do these differences affect our working together as a team?

8. How can and do these differences affect our overall productivity?

9. What policies and procedures inhibit you from doing your absolute best work?

10. What things am I doing that help and hinder our work together as a team?

11. What biases do you perceive I reflect?

12. What suggestions do you have for me as a manager or team leader?

These are just a few questions to get you and your diverse work team on an inclusive path for performance.

From a behavioral standpoint, managers must also project a positive self-fulfilling prophecy with others that reflects trust, confidence, and appreciation for the value they bring to the workplace. The implications of the self-fulfilling prophecy in the workplace are dramatic. Because of the stereotypical cultural programming we have all been raised with, we may unknowingly project self-fulfilling prophecies onto others that actually wind up occurring in the workplace.

For example, it might be assumed that traditional employees are competent and more effective workers and that employees from other groups might be less competent until proven other-wise. The manager's role is critical in this dynamic process because he or she has the authority to give or withhold rewards. If we assume that a person will fail, they often do—largely as a result of the negative climate, lower expectations, and impact on the individual's motivation level. When we truly believe that an employee is capable and our behavior is congruent with that assumption, employees often become motivated to show us that we are not wrong. As an effective manager of diversity, it is better to assume that people are competent and will succeed, until they prove otherwise. The self-fulfilling prophecy is particularly important with non-traditional employees, because the traditional work environment has automatically assumed that individuals from these groups are less competent, thus putting them at an immediate disadvantage.

Managing Diversity: A Learning Process

In summary, we know that developing competency to effectively manage diversity is a continuous learning process. It requires self-awareness, knowledge, understanding, and behavior changes that value others for who they are, not what we want them to be. To do this effectively, here are a few ideas to get you started:

Know your own culture (values, beliefs, assumptions):

❖ Reflect on your early life experiences, and those significant emotional events that have shaped your value system and your beliefs and attitudes about those who are different from you. Answer relevant questions such as What formative influences have shaped your points of view? Place of origin? Family structure? Socioeconomic status? Religion? Education?

❖ Keep a journal. Carefully note your reactions to current world events and news reports, and describe and analyze your interactions with others.

❖ Enroll in courses that examine and discuss cultures, values, and beliefs.

Know your own limitations (strengths and weaknesses):

❖ Request—and really listen to—feedback from multiple sources about your strengths and weaknesses. And be sure to get such feedback only from people you are sure will "tell it like it is," not from those who will merely tell you what you want to hear. In particular, try to get feedback from people who are from a different race or gender.

❖ Seek out those experiences that will enable you to practice your strengths and shore up your weaknesses.

❖ Change whatever you can about yourself, and accept whatever you can't, or won't. But above all, be very aware of the consequences, for better or worse, of changing or not changing.

Practice empathy with each other:

❖ Develop friendships and relationships with as many people from as many diverse backgrounds as you can, not only at work but outside of work as well.

❖ Listen closely to the views of those friends and acquaintances and work hard to understand them, especially if these world views differ widely from your own.

❖ Join organizations that expressly seek to advance the interests of different race and gender groups.

Respect other cultures:

❖ Cultivate friendships with people from as many cultures as possible.

❖ Don't rush to judgment when it comes to areas of cultural difference. Values are not necessarily better or worse than one another, but can simply reflect a cherishing of our differences.

❖ When judging others' cultural values and norms, refrain from using only your "yardstick."

❖ Continually ask yourself whether you are making a value judgment about others, rather than recognizing that others might simply have different ways of reaching their goals.

Learn by interacting:

❖ Join associations that deal specifically with the concerns of a particular race or gender.

❖ Pay close attention to the way others react to your behavior.

❖ When uncertain as to just what those reactions of others might mean, simply ask them and fully absorb their responses without second guessing them.

Strive to be nonjudgmental:

❖ Try to understand the hidden dynamics of your interactions with others, rather than merely pretend that frictions don't exist.

❖ Remember that evolution has programmed our brains to make snap judgments; learn to work with that tendency in order to rise above it.

❖ Remember that your own culture is only one standard when it comes to assessing cultural norms and values.

❖ Acknowledge frankly that whenever we make snap judgments about an event or a person, it invariably does affect our next encounter with them.

Be aware of your stereotypes:

❖ Recognize that while stereotyping is normal, it is dangerous. And understand that while the brain and mind stereotype, we have the opportunity to frankly acknowledge that fact and prevent it from showing up in our behavior.

❖ Develop relationships with people of other racial or ethnic groups, and with people of the opposite gender.

❖ Enter freely and without inhibition into learning situations where stereotypes are openly identified and confronted.

❖ Ask people you trust to gently challenge you if they believe you have used a stereotype in making a judgment.

Learn how to communicate effectively and compassionately:

❖ Practice speaking directly, candidly, and clearly, but also tactfully and compassionately.

❖ Listen actively; paraphrase what the other person has said and then ask him or her whether your paraphrase is an accurate version of what he or she was trying to convey.

❖ Continually check and recheck your perceptions, asking yourself whether your interpretations of behavior and non-verbal signals have been valid.

Listen closely, and observe carefully:

❖ Ask probing questions to help you distinguish between what someone actually has said or done and your own reactions to or judgments about it.

❖ Ask those you trust to gently challenge you on those occasions when you seemed to be listening, but really were not.

❖ Consider talking less and thinking and listening more.

❖ Develop your powers of observation by taking part in workshops where trained facilitators will give you immediate feedback as to your awareness or lack of it.

❖ Enter into a no-holds-barred discussion about work situations with people you trust of both genders and of different racial and ethnic backgrounds.

Strive to relate meaningfully to those you perceive as "different":

❖ Recognize that the entire organization must continually strive to understand, value, respect, and appreciate differences if the organization is to be more competitive.

❖ Understand that complementary skills and strengths promote a higher level of quality in terms of tasks, products, and relationships.

Be flexible; learn how to adapt:

❖ Spend some time with people from diverse cultures, both at work and outside of work.

❖ Consciously seek out knowledge and experience relating to different cultures and people to expand your own range of options and choices.

❖ Read publications that express viewpoints that differ from your own.

❖ Travel to experience other peoples' cultures in their surroundings rather than your own.

Adjust yourself according to people's reactions:

❖ Solicit feedback from as many different sources as possible.

❖ Practice adjusting your behavior in response to that feedback, then request more feedback on your adjustments.

Learn how to live with ambiguity:

❖ Seek out situations, both at work and outside of work, that induce discomfort; then find ways of raising your comfort level.

❖ Solicit guidance as to the appropriate behavior when you find yourself in ambiguous circumstances.

Be as consistent as you can be, without becoming inflexible:

❖ Solicit feedback from a variety of people at work and outside of work who have had a chance to observe you with opportunities to deal with unfamiliar situations (Fernandez, 1999).

This chapter has presented you with some tools and techniques to help you develop competencies for effectively managing diversity. If you and your organization strive to be effective in the global marketplace, it is imperative that you maintain personal and system-wide accountability for your awareness, knowledge, and actions. Your individual success and the organization's success depend on it!

References

Adler, N. J., & Kiggunder, M. K. (1983). "Awareness at the crossroad: Designing translator-based training programs," in *Handbook of intercultural training*, Vol. II. Don Landes and Richard Breslin. New York: Pergamon.

Carnevale, A. P., & Kogod, K. S. (1996). *Tools and activities for a diverse work force.* New York: McGraw-Hill. Contributing article by Gardenswartz, L. & Rowe, A. (1994). *Management development diversity needs analysis: awareness, knowledge, and skills*, p. 147. New York: Irwin.

Carnevale, A. P., & Kogod, K. S. (1996). *Tools and activities for a diverse work force.* New York: McGraw-Hill. Contributing article by Deane, B. *Skills for managing diverse people: Making a list*, pp. 228–231. Seattle, WA: The GilDeane Group.

Fernandez, J. P. (1999). *Race, gender and rhetoric.* New York: McGraw-Hill.

Gardenswartz, L., & Rowe, A. (1994). *The managing diversity survival guide.* Boston: McGraw-Hill.

Hubbard, E. E. (2002). *Techniques for managing a diverse workforce.* Petaluma, CA: Global Insights Publishing.

Mendez-Russell, A.; Wilderson Jr., F., Ph.D.; & Tolbert, A.S., Ph.D. (1994). *Discovering diversity profile.* Minneapolis, MN: Carlson Learning Company.

Rasmussen, T. (1996). *The ASTD trainer's sourcebook: Diversity.* New York: McGraw-Hill.

Thomas, R. R. (2001). From affirmative action to affirming diversity. *Harvard Business Review on Managing Diversity.* Boston: Harvard Business School Press, pp. 1–32.

Zemke, R., Raines, C., & Filipczak, B. (2000). *Generations at work.* New York: AMACOM.

Chapter 6
Workplace Applications

Introduction

Diversity is a challenge that has the potential to be either a positive or a negative influence on an organization. Ignoring the fact that diversity exists and treating all people as if there are no differences between them will grossly underutilize a critical asset of the organization. Consider the following: "Diversity is not only about 'representation,' it is about 'utilization'!" "It's not about counting heads, but making heads count!" In order for diversity to have a positive effect, a manager's awareness, knowledge, understanding, and behavior must be combined to create specific actions to capitalize on and leverage the power of diversity. Otherwise, this valuable resource will go untapped.

Diversity can be leveraged in a wide variety of areas throughout the organization. In this chapter, we will examine how diversity strategies can be applied to

- ❖ Recruitment/Selection
- ❖ Employee Retention and Development
- ❖ Team Building
- ❖ Customer Service
- ❖ Improving Market Share

Recruitment/Selection

Recruitment and selection is often the first place organizations will start when building a diverse work environment. Oftentimes, however, many organizations demonstrate only a superficial commitment to diversity in spite of demographic and other evidence to the contrary. A common refrain heard by many goes something like this: "If only we could find some truly qualified women and minorities, we would be happy to hire them. Those folks don't seem to be interested in the type of work we do in our industry. If you find some, we'll hire them."

In reality, this type of statement at best is an unfounded assertion and at its worst reflects another form of racism and sexism that stems from cultural programming that has effectively gone unchallenged. Qualified women and minorities are certainly out there if the work environment and the job offers are right. There's no secret in finding them; however, organizations need to rely on diverse recruitment people and diverse approaches to attract and retain a diverse workforce. It's simply a matter of committing the organization to developing systematic, objective, rational, and fair recruiting strategies, implementing those strategies aggressively, and fostering a team environment that treats people fairly, regardless of their differences.

The current changing landscape of American demographics, both native and foreign born, reflects a labor pool that comprises a large population of educated, capable people from diverse backgrounds, especially in the high-tech and service-based industries. Any U.S. organization that desires to stay competitive for now and in the future is going to have to find, recruit, and retain the best employees, regardless of their diverse backgrounds. Too often, recruiters and their organizations evaluate new recruits solely on the basis of how they "fit" the organization's culture, which is somewhat antiquated in today's hiring practices and requirements (today, many organizations try to avoid hiring in their own image). Many of these interviews are unstructured and haphazard; the interviewers are often poorly trained in how to conduct a "culture-fair," objective interview. And, there are very few metrics and incentives that encourage the interviewers to make certain they obtain a diverse candidate pool.

To be effective, recruiters and their organizations should look at a potential employee's intellectual, technical, and professional skills and at their desire, their understanding of their personal culture, their strengths and weaknesses, their emotional intelligence, their ability to be empathetic, and their willingness to accept and value different race, ethnic, and gender groups. Recruiters, interviewers, and hiring managers need effective tools to help them make good decisions regarding the best person for the job given *all* of the human resources available without the hindrance of bias. The steps in Figure 6-1 can be helpful in avoiding race and gender bias in the recruitment and hiring process.

Figure 6-1. Steps to Avoid Race and Gender Bias

Step	Activity
1	**Develop specific selection criteria**. It is essential to develop specific hiring criteria and to make sure that all the interviewers and hiring managers make use of them.
2	**Develop specific instruments to measure the criteria.** Everyone in the interviewing and hiring process should be using them. A matrix usually works well as a summary tool. List the candidates down the left side and the criteria across the top row. For each cell created, enter the candidate's response on each criterion listed. In this way, you can compare their responses against the same criteria.
3	**Train interviewers.** Interviewers need to go through their own self-analysis to examine their own culture, norms, values, emotional intelligence, racial and gender attitudes, and the like. They should go through the recruitment process, just like any other new job candidate. And they should receive feedback from recruits about their skills.
4	**Have diverse interviewers.** Because of our natural tendency to hire people like ourselves, it is crucial that women and minorities be recruiters and interviewers.
5	**Use a team approach.** All parties to the process should meet as a team to review candidates and to arrive at a team decision.
6	**Evaluate the recruiters.** Recruiters should be evaluated in terms of their number of hires as well as of the race and gender, type of positions, and the success or failure of their recruits.

Developing College Connections

A number of organizations have recognized that soon the United States will experience a "birth dearth" period based on

Census data. That is, due to the lack of births in recent years, there will be a 27.9 percent reduction in the talent available for work over an 18-year period. During that 18-year period, there will be a 7-year "drought" period. Because of this and other labor shortage issues, more and more organizations are acknowledging their need for a systematic, year-round college relations program that can begin to woo candidates from all backgrounds when they are just starting their educational careers. The following are some key elements of an effective college relations program:

1. Evaluate and select a limited number of specific schools that have a good track record in terms of producing diverse talent that matches your organization's present and future needs, especially those colleges that have high populations of each targeted demographic group.

2. Dedicate to each college a diverse team headed by a senior officer.

3. Train team members in their roles, and include diversity and multicultural interviewing training on an ongoing basis.

4. Maintain a year-round presence at the college; don't just show up at recruitment time, when most likely the best candidates already have been snapped up anyway.

5. Evaluate the teams in terms of their success or failure in attracting women and minority candidates.

6. Create and review your recruitment success metrics and publish the results to the rest of the organization.

When your diverse recruitment teams are planning on-campus strategies to create an effective approach, the actions in Figure 6-2 can be taken to improve their hit rate.

Figure 6-2. On-Campus Strategies Checklist

✓	Activity
	Have formal and informal lunches and dinners with key students, faculty members, and administrators.
	Seek out and develop relationships with various student clubs and professional associations, such as Historically Black Colleges and Universities (HBCU), Hispanic Association of Colleges and Universities (HACU), Catalyst (Women's Organization), INROADS (Inner City and Youth Development Organization), and others. Don't forget the organizations on campus that are devoted to meeting the needs of part-time, returning, and evening students.
	Volunteer to personally give lectures and conduct classes, and/or recruit some suitable employees who are not on the team to help you out in this regard.
	Support student activities, and provide financial help as part of your organization's community development effort. This will help bolster the organization's image on campus.
	Provide year-round, ongoing internships for students, and get the jump on other organizations by letting them begin in their senior year of high school.
	Provide a "Step Ahead" program for students—where students work in the organization during their summer vacation and other short periods of time (when school is out during other periods). Be sure that they get real experience on projects of substance, not just used as an extra pair of hands in the mailroom. Have their projects end with a written or an oral report. This allows them to summarize and demonstrate their on-the-job learning.

It is also critical to have strategies to recruit existing seasoned employees to fill positions at all levels. Organizations can't afford to overlook the recruitment of experienced employees to fill key strategic positions within the organization. Here are just a few ideas to get you started:

❖ Develop contacts with stakeholders from diverse backgrounds.

❖ Develop relationships with local and national religious, professional, political, and social organizations whose focus is people from diverse groups.

❖ Locate and develop relationships with recruitment firms dedicated to diverse groups.

❖ Develop a recruitment directory that contains listings for people from women and minority search firms, colleges and universities, sororities, fraternities, professional and political associations, community organizations, publications to advertise in, and vocational and technical schools.

❖ Remember, this is not about quotas. It is about finding the person who is best qualified for the job given *all* the talent pools available.

When you talk with diverse groups during the recruiting process, don't be surprised if they are skeptical. Based on different experiences, they may want to check out the organization to see if it is diversity friendly. They may ask questions such as those in Figure 6-3, which you must be prepared to answer or demonstrate in your behavior during the recruitment process.

Recruiting for a highly successful diverse workforce involves developing a vision for building and supporting a diverse workforce in your organization. This includes considering how you recruit both internally and externally.

Figure 6-3. Diversity-Friendly Environment Question Check/Preparation List

✓	Questions
	How many women and minorities hold senior positions in the company?
	What is the company's philosophy of and commitment to developing women and minorities?
	What is the level of commitment of the organization to diversity and Affirmative Action?
	How has the organization handled charges of discrimination in the past?
	How sensitive, aware, and comfortable are interviewers with candidates of diverse backgrounds?
	How honest, straightforward, and candid are interviewers during the recruitment process?
	To what extent does the company keep the commitments it makes throughout the recruitment process.
	How do other women and minorities view the organization?
	How does the community perceive the organization's reputation and involvement.
	What is the organization's attitude regarding employees balancing work and personal life?

Internal Recruiting

Left on its own, internal recruiting usually occurs without much thought given to issues of utilizing the diversity that exists within the organization unless there is a clear commitment to building and supporting a diverse work environment. There often seems to be a disproportionate number of people of color, women, people with disabilities, etc., in front-line worker positions versus management positions. There are both pros and cons to internal recruiting.

On the one hand, promoting from within is very cost-effective and can boost morale by letting employees know that hard work does pay off in opportunities for growth and development. One of the downsides of internal recruiting is that your organization can miss the opportunity to bring in fresh new talent with new perspectives and approaches. Another downside of internal recruiting is that the organization can become wrapped up in its own organizational programming that it stagnates due to excessive inbreeding of ideas and processes. An inbred organization may approach problem solving and operational processes with tunnel vision. In addition, any new ideas that suggest changes and innovation may meet head on with resistance.

An effective internal recruiting process will take into account the following internal resources:

❖ **Promotions.** Examine your leadership development, specialized technical, and general managerial programs to locate candidates. This is a good place to assess whether or not your diversity efforts are working. Conduct a demographic analysis of the makeup of these groups. Do they include women and minorities, or people who are a part of an underrepresented group? How often have these programs graduated someone who is a part of a diverse group? What support programs have been put in place to help ensure a successful start?

❖ **Transfers.** "Job shadowing" opportunities can enhance learning and impact career choices. When this is done, however, it is critical to make certain the climate the transferee will experience is a positive one. The transfer group may need some diversity training before they are left to operate on their own.

❖ **Work Teams.** Work teams need diversity training as well. Simply because a team contains members with diverse backgrounds does not make them effective. Remember, diversity is about utilization, not representation. These teams can be another source of talent.

❖ **Committee.** Reviewing members who are a part of special committees can also be a source of possible talent for growth. This assumes that the process for accessing these committees is open to a variety of members from diverse backgrounds. In many cases, selection to participate on these committees can be tantamount to promotion and even succession. In some organizations, women and minorities rarely get nominated as part of the committee selection process.

External Recruiting

External recruiting is often well organized, having a systematic and consistent approach. Many organizations use the same resources to draw new employees year after year. The unspoken belief may be "If it's not broken, why fix it?" The flaw in this type of thinking is that if you don't seek out new resources, you will not diversify your applicant pool. The challenge here is to expand your horizons and seek out additional and perhaps non-traditional sources of applicants.

As with internal recruiting, there are both pros and cons to external recruiting. If your organization is actively seeking a skill set that is not available internally, it is to your benefit to look outside. Also, if you are trying to improve your organization's diversity mixture, there is a larger pool of candidates outside. However, keep in mind that there are consequences involved. Employees who do not get promotional opportunities are left wondering, "Why not me?" They might not see the skill and qualification differences being brought in from the outside. This is made worse when this same employee is asked to show the new person how things should operate. Loss of morale, loyalty, and satisfaction can be the result of this action.

Be sure to make use of some of the following recruiting channels that involve traditional and non-traditional sources as well as to create specialized lists of your own:

- ❖ Chamber of Commerce
- ❖ Church activities
- ❖ Sporting events
- ❖ Community organizations
- ❖ Family and friends of diverse groups (employee referrals)
- ❖ Career days
- ❖ Disabled student services
- ❖ Corporate-sponsored events that are diversity focused
- ❖ Service providers that have access to diverse groups
- ❖ Using multi-cultured media advertisements

Potential employees will usually get their first look at the organization based on your recruitment efforts and media exposure. It is one of the best places to start to apply your skills to build a diverse work environment.

Employee Retention and Development

In addition to recruiting a diverse workforce, there must be processes in place to retain and develop employees. The ability to retain the diverse work group once they have been recruited is a critical management competency. It helps avoid "human capital depletion" and "revolving-door impact." Some organizations do a wonderful job setting up systems to recruit diverse employees, only to lose them 12 to 18 months later in voluntary turnover (human capital depletion). This often occurs because there is little thought given to retaining them once they are inside the organization. If this happens, they show up in the "revolving-door" statistics (poor survival rate).

Making a commitment to diversity means more than striving for immediate results such as improved demographics. Employees must feel welcomed and supported. They need to know that the organization has systems, processes, and people in place to help give them the best possible chance for success and allow them to build an invigorating career.

Training programs are one form of development; however, training programs alone are not enough to keep employees for the long run. Employee retention and development must be a complete, comprehensive system that includes processes and systems such as

❖ Coaching and counseling

❖ Career planning

❖ Mentoring

❖ Succession planning

❖ Performance rating equity analysis

❖ Compensation equity analysis

❖ Diversity-friendly policies and procedures

The processes and techniques listed in Figure 6-4 can be used to improve employee retention and development.

Figure 6-4. Employee Retention and Development Idea List

✓	Activity
	Create a ***pre-recruitment training*** program designed to tackle issues concerning lack of information about available jobs, diverse candidates' lack of confidence, poor interview skills, etc.
	Review job vacancies to make certain that individual preferences ***are not*** being substituted for real job requirements.
	Solicit ideas from recent hires and current employees who represent diverse groups regarding potential sources of candidates for hiring slates.
	Help sponsor an internship for women, people of color, and other underrepresented groups (age, people with disabilities, protected classes, etc.).

(continued)

Figure 6-4. Employee Retention and Development Idea List *(continued)*

✓	Activity
	Attend or sponsor career fairs or "recruiting rallies" focused on women and people of color, and serve as an interviewer. Offer development seminars covering different subjects such as "Developing Professional Selling Skills, Interviewing Skills, Etiquette, Benefits—Your Hidden Paycheck" and Diversity in the Workplace.
	Review all slates for hires, promotions, and laterals to ensure their diversity balance.
	Commit a full-time resource to address recruitment for women and people of color.
	Provide and obtain timely and specific performance feedback.
	Create methods to analyze the reasons—as given by employees and their managers—for losses of women and people of color by level. Check for themes and patterns to take corrective action.
	If women and/or people of color have voluntarily left the organization, *make certain that exit interviews are conducted prior to their departure and six months later.* If possible, the exit interviews should be conducted by an external third party. The later time period and third party interviewers reduce inhibitions to criticize an ex-employer for fear of reprisal.

(continued)

Figure 6-4. Employee Retention and Development Idea List *(concluded)*

✓	Activity
	Create assessments (e.g., targeted survey, focus groups) to determine if women and people of color feel their talents, skills, and abilities are underutilized.
	Create an assessment (e.g., targeted survey, focus groups) to determine if women and people of color feel they have been given sufficient responsibility and authority to make decisions within their current organization.
	Conduct mentoring programs for high potential women and minorities. Also use "reverse mentoring"—having mentors working with others who are different from themselves.
	Assign a peer-coach to new hires. A peer-coach is a person who is available to a new hire to answer questions, help them navigate the culture and systems of the organization, introduce them to others, and help bridge their transition to the workplace.
	Create skill development and cross-training opportunities like job-sharing or placing diverse employees in charge while you are on vacation or on special assignment for your own development.

One of the primary goals of retention and development processes is to develop employees so that they can do their absolute personal best work and will want to remain with the organization to build a career. It becomes expensive for organizations when this goal is not achieved.

For those looking for hard numbers to support the value of diversity, an obvious place to start looking is to examine the organization's turnover and productivity numbers. Each year, organizations spend millions of dollars recruiting and training employees. When an employee experiences a poor, unwelcoming work environment, he or she gets the message pretty clearly: "This company may be a nice place to train, but you wouldn't want to work here." So they don't; they usually wind up leaving the organization. In these cases, diverse workforce turnover can become a serious problem. As a result, the organization pays the price of turnover that is on average 1.5 times the salary of the person who leaves, and that's just to get them in the door! This represents a poor return on investment for the organization.

Even when turnover is relatively low, the unwillingness of an organization to step up to the issue of valuing diversity can lower morale and productivity. In the competitive business environment of today, organizations simply cannot afford to sacrifice any level of productivity. Even marginal declines in productivity can put an organization in serious jeopardy of losing some portion of their competitive advantage (Loden, 1996).

The approaches shown here are just a few examples of techniques you can use to help you manage and improve the retention of your diverse workforce.

Team Building

One of the greatest benefits to an organization of encouraging diversity in a business improvement context is the outcome of using diverse work teams. As mentioned earlier, using diverse work groups effectively is not an automatic occurrence; one cannot simply put people who are different in the same room and expect beneficial results. Managers must help the group go through a distinct process of personal and group identity change if the value they bring to the organization will be realized.

You must help team members understand the value of the differences that each member brings to the team. As team members, they will meet and constantly work with others whose cultures may differ considerably from their own. When team members meet for the first time, they will typically base their impressions on one another's physical appearance, facial features, skin color, hair, stature, dress, mannerisms, voice tone, etc. However, after working together, they have the opportunity to learn about each other at a deeper level and not be influenced by their first impressions only. They may notice different behaviors that seem awkward and/or peculiar or difficult to understand. They might often need your help in utilizing your knowledge (and the development of their own) of cultural differences to make them more comfortable. In essence, you will help them bridge the cultural differences gap to construct a foundation for future learning.

Selma G. Myers has developed a *Team Development Model* that suggests that although traditional teams will go through the five stages listed on pages 131–133, diverse work groups go through these stages differently and will deal with issues that might not come up or be as unsettling in homogeneous groups (Myers, 1996).

Driving Stage

This stage involves the team in focusing on its mission, goals, priorities, and guidelines. However, while some cultural groups are comfortable in a structured environment, other groups may not be. When you add dynamics such as language (i.e., English is not the first language of some of the members and they find it difficult to comprehend), different values around time, variations in norms regarding group interaction, and viewpoints on authority, it changes the speed with which the group can move forward and can affect their development if it is not handled well.

Strive Stage

This stage involves moving ahead with full understanding and agreement on roles and responsibilities. However, some cultural groups have great interest in gaining more responsibility, while others are not as open to taking on responsibility without formal support such as rank, age, etc. Some individuals might be very open to the concept of change, while others are satisfied with the status quo.

Thrive Stage

This stage involves rapid growth involving peer feedback, conflict management, and decision making. However, various cultural groups might have different approaches to communication and conflict, and reach decisions in a number of different ways. For example, certain cultures value directness and frankness in interpersonal communication, while others place a high value on subtlety in their communication style.

Arrive Stage

This stage involves peak performance, where all the factors are in sync. Finally, the team has arrived when all members have been recognized, appreciated, accepted, encouraged, and acknowledged for the strengths they bring to the team, in a way that is consistent with their culture.

Revive Stage

This stage involves regaining peak performance when slippage in team performance occurs, when the team memberships change, or when the team's mandate or purpose has changed. At this stage, the interaction between members of the diverse team needs to be reexamined. Blaming without recognizing cultural differences is counterproductive. When knowledge of cultural differences is used effectively, team members remain open-minded and motivated, and support each other to attain peak performance again.

In order for diverse work teams to be effective, the characteristics listed in Figure 6-5 must be in place.

Figure 6-5. Effective Diversity Work Team Characteristics

✓	Key Components
	A strong mission or purpose. Team members might disagree about many things and have vigorous disputes with one another; however, when they have an overarching mission or purpose that is compelling and transcends cultural barriers (such as building an inclusive work environment that works for all of us), the team finds a way to work together. Diverse work teams want to know that they have a role to play that is valued and that they have a stake in the outcome.

(continued)

133

Figure 6-5. Effective Diversity Work Team Characteristics *(continued)*

✓	Key Components
	A clearly defined performance outcome. No matter what type of team you have (diverse or traditional), it is critical that the members of the team have a clear and well-defined performance outcome that creates a "line-of-sight" understanding of their work and how it adds value to the organization. The team's performance outcome(s) must be measurable, specific, and time-bound for which the team can be held accountable. It is difficult to drum up excitement and support for an outcome that is ill defined.
	An understanding of different cultural norms and their impact on team communication, problem solving, and conflict. U.S. cultural norms tend to favor analytical over intuitive problem solving and favor directness over avoidance in conflict management. This is certainly not the case in other cultures and in a diverse team; the lack of sensitivity to these kinds of issues can spell disaster and breed dysfunction. In some non-U.S.–based cultures, ethnic groups prize harmonious interactions when dealing with differences and use communication strategies that keep the conversations purposely vague and indirect. Understanding these norms is critical to a diverse work team's functioning at both a personal and group level. If synergy is to develop, the team and its leader must be knowledgeable and skilled in the use of "cultural frames of reference" to help create team solutions.
	A set of shared values that clearly articulate demonstrations of dignity and respect. Everyone wants to be valued and treated with respect and dignity.

(continued)

Figure 6-5. Effective Diversity Work Team Characteristics *(continued)*

✓	Key Components
	What is unclear is the way each culture wants to be valued and respected, and the ways that show they have been treated with dignity. What measures should be used? One of the early exercises in the team's development (in the Driving Stage) should focus on identifying the elements that constitute a respectful way for the team to operate. We certainly are aware of the costs if this is not done: Teams disintegrate and become groups unable to adapt, or worse yet, poorly focused and frustrated individuals.
	A cultivation of different points of view. Diverse work teams deal with their diversity much more easily and flexibly when they embrace differences by following the principle of "no fewer than three points of view." This rule instills the belief that there is no best way and that the more options you have, the better your potential solutions are. Just legalizing the notion that things aren't "either-or" sets up a norm and value in the team that identifying different approaches from different perspectives and judging them on their value to the stated need open up everyone's thinking to exploration.
	A willingness to do what it takes to get the job done. A key ingredient for excellence in the team is each team member's commitment to being accountable for his or her assigned tasks and working with others interactively and cooperatively until the job is done. Team members make certain that all members cross the finish line together, handling obstacles and

(continued)

Figure 6-5. Effective Diversity Work Team Characteristics *(continued)*

✓	Key Components
	providing support as needed. Contribution is measured by what the team is able to accomplish, and improved performance is assessed by how well the team can collectively implement changes and perform. The task does not go unfinished, nor does a member get left behind.
	Loyalty and devotion to the team experience. Loyalty and particularly devotion are strong words and are rarely mentioned as a necessity when discussing team performance. Nevertheless, they are important because they imply passion and energy, not just run-of-the-mill work. It is possible to accomplish a task without true devotion to the whole experience; however, the end result might leave a lot to be desired. For some cultures, this level of passion and devotion to the outcome is a driving force.
	A desire for individual and collective growth. Part of the intrigue and frustration of a diverse work team process is that you have to merge your skills, competencies, ideas, values, and priorities with others. Figuring out how to do that well is a complex process that requires tenacity. Although a diverse work team members' skills and knowledge might be complementary and not necessarily conflicting, aligning priorities, making decisions, and solving problems frequently expose areas of friction in the team. The individual and exponential growth of the team and its members will depend on the team's ability to work through these "frictional moments of truth." Some teams are nearly

(continued)

Figure 6-5. Effective Diversity Work Team Characteristics *(concluded)*

✓	Key Components
	pushed to the breaking point when these frictional moments occur. It is what they do in these moments along with their cultural knowledge base and processes agreed to ahead of time that determine if the team truly learns from the situation and acquires the skills needed to handle any other present or future conflicts. This is an ongoing competency-building process that if mastered, creates a significant operational and competitive advantage for the organization.
	An openness to new experiences and processes, both interpersonal and problem solving. Learning can't enter through a closed mind. Being a life-long learner and open to new experiences goes a long way toward effectively working with and accepting others who are different. There is a saying that states once your mind is stretched with a new idea, it never goes back to the same shape. You take that knowledge with you. Diverse work teams, if properly managed, can allow all members of the team to grow and develop.
	Shared laughter and humor as an integral part of the team experience. While having fun as teammates in the process of accomplishing a task is not absolutely necessary, it adds immeasurably to the experience of working together. In fact, it is an important determinant in creating more tenacity and follow-through in meeting the team's performance objectives. Oftentimes, teams will notice how much their quality and productivity were enhanced, not sacrificed, through their laughter and that it made the team experience one they want to repeat.

Customer Service and Improving Market Share

When it comes to addressing issues of diversity's link to the financial bottom line, one of the most compelling yet under-used and least leveraged arguments is diversity's link and connection to customer service and satisfaction for both internal and external customers. Unfortunately, managers and even some diversity practitioners have not gotten this connection. Some who do get it, do not try to help their organization see this connection. The connection appears to be pretty straight-forward.

If an organization does not foster a culture of understanding, respect, and cooperation, the ability of the workforce can be severely limited in effectively interacting with the diverse customers of the organization. Organizations often like to stay close to and focus on the customer; however, there is a high probability that your employees are marketing to, selling to, and interacting with your customers based on outdated assumptions, personal biases, inaccurate stereotypes, and dis-respectful behaviors due to their cultural programming. If the organization has a high incidence of internal harassment complaints, can it feel confident that this is not a customer service issue as well? If employees are uncomfortable dealing with their openly gay co-workers, are they likely to be effective and respectful when dealing with customers who are open about their sexual orientation? In addition, are they likely to aggressively go after important, strategic business opportunities with this group or any group they might have a bias against?

Whether sanctioned by the organization or not, discriminatory practices are always costly. While some might not lead to multi-million dollar lawsuits, they do tarnish the image and brand reputation of an organization in the eyes of customers, investors, and potential employees. It can lead to lost sales, boycotts, and legal judgments that cost the organization millions of dollars in lost revenues, management, and legal costs.

Organizations intent on leveraging diversity in their marketplace must also understand the particular consumer preferences of their diverse customers. Major corporations such as Nike, Ford, McDonald's, and Coca-Cola are going all out to win over free-spending ethnic consumers by recruiting minority marketing experts who speak each group's language and know their customs. Mass marketing is a relic of the past when America was a cultural melting pot. Today you need a different message to suit the taste of each group. With databased marketing techniques becoming more sophisticated, diverse market segments are easier to identify. Once identified, it is possible to appeal to many segments in separate and distinct ways, provided the organization does its homework to develop a depth of knowledge on each targeted group and build relationships with them as customers based on the way they want to be treated and "sold to." In addition, you have to "sell your work" to internal customers who are different from yourself. Your effectiveness will be determined by your ability to communicate across differences. No matter who the customer is, the more knowledge you acquire about the customer, the more likely you will be successful in customizing and personalizing an approach that meets that customer's needs.

In many cases, successfully selling to diverse markets will require identifying the obstacles that stand in the way of the organization building effective cross-cultural relationships with its customers. The organization's characteristics and the customer's unique background will determine what obstacles need to be overcome and the correct strategies to do so. If not done well, there are a number of disastrous consequences that can happen for failing to take the time to know your market. Here are just a few well-publicized examples:

❖ In Hong Kong, a car rental company unsuccessfully attempted to promote itself by giving away green hats. The company was unaware of the Chinese superstition that if a man wears a green hat, his wife is cheating on him!

❖ In Japan, a manufacturer of golf balls failed in an effort to market its product by selling the balls in packages of four. The manufacturer was unaware that in Japan, there are negative connotations associated with the number four and with items grouped in four. The manufacturer failed to get acquainted with its market and thus failed to respect a cultural difference.

According to Fernandez (1999), there are seven obstacles to cross-cultural marketing relationships and seven steps to achieving an effective target market strategy, as described in Figure 6-6.

If these obstacles are to be overcome, Fernandez (1999) suggests that a combination of internally and externally focused initiatives will have to be undertaken. In combination, these initiatives, listed in Figure 6-7, will help support the development of a target market strategy that is capable of delivering value plus products and services over the short and long term.

Figure 6-6. Seven Obstacles to Cross-Cultural Marketing Relationships

	Obstacles
1	Assuming that the entire target market segment is homogeneous; that is, assuming that all members of that market have identical values, beliefs, assumptions, preferences, wants, and needs.
2	Conducting little or no research into the wants, needs, and culture of the targeted segment, but instead relying merely on gut feelings and stereotypes.
3	Erroneously believing that one can reach a targeted market segment through only one marketing method (e.g., assuming that all Hispanics can be reached through television, when in fact Spanish-language radio might be the more effective method).
4	Erroneously believing that a mass marketing strategy such as advertising can be quickly and painlessly adapted to a target market merely by translating it into that target market's preferred language.
5	Creating advertisements that are out of sync with the mood, values, and/or culture of the target market.
6	Placing advertisements only in mass-market publications rather than also utilizing publications geared directly toward the target market.
7	Blindly and expensively developing new products and services on the basis of an unexamined assumption that the current product and service mix does not meet the targeted segment's needs and wants.

Figure 6-7. Seven Steps Toward an Effective Target Market Strategy

Step	Key Strategies
1	Understand your own and your organization's culture.
2	Understand the target market's culture.
3	Identify key stakeholder groups.
4	Develop relationships based on trust and respect; become a proactive community citizen.
5	Identify market segment needs, preference, and expectations through a variety of methods, such as interviews and focus groups.
6	Develop products, services, and delivery mechanisms that will deliver value-added products to customers.
7	Continually check up on your progress, and ask members of the target market to provide you with ongoing feedback.

The example below shows how the use of these steps can improve your marketplace effectiveness. To illustrate Step 2: Understand the target market's culture, we will examine a situation from Southern New England Telephone.

Southern New England Telephone took the time to understand why its Hispanic accounts had a much higher delinquency rate than its other accounts. What it discovered was that many aspects of Hispanic culture were directly clashing with its customer service system. For example, the average Hispanic customers felt a need to develop rapport with a customer service representative before he or she was comfortable getting down to business. The abrupt style that SNET had taught its reps caused many Hispanics to feel alienated and hesitant to call the company to work out a problem. SNET also found that their policy of not accepting third-party checks or cash payments made it difficult for Hispanic customers to pay their bills and that using only English on their bills made it difficult for many Hispanic customers to understand them. Therefore, you can see how, by simply making an effort to get to know the culture and needs of their Hispanic customers, SNET was able to significantly lower its delinquency rates.

Another example involves General Motors.

In 1996, General Motors won a $1 billion automotive deal with China, in large part because back in 1986 it had hired a very prominent, American-born Chinese woman who was well connected in China. In addition, they had a company support (affinity) group for Asians. Therefore, the company's knowledge of China, its culture, and some key contacts gave GM an advantage over the other major car manufacturers who were pursuing the same contract.

Still, another example:

Acknowledging that its products weren't selling well in Asia, Bausch & Lomb turned to its Asian employees for guidance. Their inquiries led them to the discovery that

Bausch & Lomb glasses weren't properly fitting Asian people. Sales rose once the company modified its glasses for its Asian markets.

As these examples and this chapter illustrate, there are a wide variety of organizational applications that support the notion that diversity is a key strategic business issue. It involves using a diverse workforce asset beyond mere representation. Whether it's recruitment and selection, employee retention and development, team building, or customer service and improving market share, a manager's job is to utilize diversity for the optimal performance of the organization and its employees.

References

Fernandez, J. P. (1999). *Race, gender, and rhetoric.* New York: McGraw-Hill.

Hubbard, E. E. (2002). *Techniques for managing a diverse workforce.* Petaluma, CA: Global Insights Publishing.

Loden, M. (1996). *Implementing diversity.* Chicago: Irwin.

Myers, S. G. (1996). *Team building for diverse work groups.* Irvine, CA: Richard Chang and Associates.

O'Mara, J. (1999). *101 actions you can take to value and manage diversity.* Castro Valley, CA: O'Mara and Associates.

Orey, M. C. (1996). *Successful staffing in a diverse workplace.* Irvine, CA: Richard Chang and Associates.

Chapter 7
Working Together
Productively

Introduction

There is no question that working together productively—
regardless of race, gender, age, etc.—is critical to the strategic
performance of an organization. Organizational performance
depends on workforce members being able to effectively
use their talents in a cohesive way that meets the business
goals and objectives of the organization. As a manager,
your role is to help create an environment where people are
able to do their best. Since "people are the organization,"
it is essential that you address the key elements that drive
productivity. These elements include but are not limited to
expectations; feedback; consequences (incentives and
sanctions); and performer skill, knowledge, and required
resources.

From a diversity perspective, diverse work group members
will have expectations that are imbedded in their cultural backgrounds. Some may have assumptions and beliefs that in order
to be effective, leaders and co-workers must be directive and
have a strong presence, whereas others are accustomed to and
expect a collaborative, consensus-building environment. To
effectively build your diversity management capability, you
need to find out what assumptions and beliefs exist within
your workforce. Understanding each team member's background and perspective is the starting point of learning how

opinions of what it is like to work in this environment as a person who is different are formed. Their assumptions and beliefs will influence how well they will work and communicate with members of the organization. To help assess your team's expectations, the worksheet in Exercise 7-1 can be used during a staff meeting to improve workforce productivity and performance.

Exercise 7-1. Productivity and Performance Worksheet

Your Views	Workforce Views	Comparison between Your Views and the Views of the Workforce	
		Similarities	Differences
My preferred meeting type is:	My diverse work group's preferred meeting type is:		
My preferred communica-tion style is:	The preferred communica-tion style of the work group given its diverse make up is:		

(continued)

Exercise 7-1. Productivity and Performance Worksheet *(concluded)*

Your Views	Workforce Views	Comparison between Your Views and the Views of the Workforce	
		Similarities	Differences
To what extent am I open to and accepting of people who are different from me?	To what extent is my work group open to and accepting of differences in each other?		
To what extent am I committed to the full utiliza-tion of our diverse work-group talent?	To what extent has my work group fully utilized the talents of each diverse work-group member?		
The primary ingredient that will make us successful as a diverse work team is:	The team's view of the primary ingre-dient that will make us suc-cessful as a diverse work group is:		

Another critical component of working together productively is managing cultural communication barriers. Linguists estimate that the 500 words used most often in the English language can produce over 14,000 meanings. And to make matters worse, those words will generally have meanings based on the direct relationship to a person's personal background and cultural experiences. Depending on the degree of dissimilarity of the sender's and the receiver's backgrounds, they will have more or less trouble understanding each other. As a person managing your diverse workforce, you must be skilled in understanding "why" this occurs and "how to help."

For nearly all of us, our opinions matter. So when disagreements occur with others, it can leave us feeling attacked and vulnerable, and cause us to become defensive and protective of our own point of view. On the receiving end, if we are not listening carefully, we might not actually hear what the other person is saying and react to the behavior we perceive as being in disagreement. This of course frustrates and disappoints the speaker, and we might interpret that frustration as hostility and respond accordingly. In the long run, the cycle continues, the misunderstandings persist, and a poor working situation is created.

If this poor communication continues over time, the listener can become frustrated and begin to label the other person or themselves as inarticulate or not worth talking to for long. This sets up a pattern for bias, prejudice, and discrimination. Depending on the individual's response to this cycle, a positive or negative environment for communication and collaborative work will arise. Let's take a look at these environmental characteristics; they often produce characteristics that are polar opposites.

Partial versus Full-bodied Listening

When we listen to someone in a full-bodied way, we not only hear the words, we pay attention to the tone and inflection, and non-verbal communication. In essence, we capture 100 percent of the message. To make certain we are really communicating, we must pay attention to whether all three elements of the sender's message—words, tone and inflection, and non-verbal or body language—are in sync. Partial listening will cause problems almost all the time. At the very least, someone in the conversation will probably walk away feeling less valued.

Indirect versus Direct Communication

In many cultures, including our own, people rarely verbalize what they truly mean or what they really feel. When this happens, our communication becomes indirect and cryptic, and puts the work team at a disadvantage because the messages are vague, distorted, or misinterpreted. We can vastly improve our communication if we work with others to learn what is needed to strengthen both the message and the reception. In addition, it must be done in a highly respectful and sensitive way.

Neutrality versus Empathy

We reassure others when we let them know we can identify with their problems, understand their feelings, and accept their emotional reactions even when we perceive them as being excessive or even hostile to us. On the other hand, whenever we deny the legitimacy of another person's emotions, what we are really doing—even when we intend to be supportive—is creating a closed, hostile environment. This fosters a breeding ground for hurt feelings, ill will, and potential charges of discrimination.

Superiority versus Equality

We certainly set off another person's defenses if we treat them with a sense of superiority that stems from the basis of race, gender ethnicity, wealth, intellectual ability, physical character-istics, and so on. The resultant feelings of inadequacy on the part of the listeners or their frustration causes them to hear only what their emotions are screaming at them to hear, and the subsequent resentment and hostility can be devastating to a diverse work team's performance.

Arrogant Certainty versus Flexibility to Learn

Some people have it all figured out, or at least they think so. They come across as knowing all the answers, needing no additional information, and regarding him- or herself as the ultimate expert or authority on everything. Anyone with this style of working is highly likely to put others on the defen-sive and will be perceived as a source of irritation. By maintaining a flexible attitude to learn and the ability to acknowledge it by saying "I don't think that way anymore," it provides a framework for growth and high performance output.

To minimize potential misunderstandings and gaps that can lead to conflict, Figure 7-1 provides a few tips for working with others who are different from you.

Figure 7-1. Effective Communication Tips to Work Productively Together

✓	Key Ideas
	Address communications issues head on in an empathetic manner. Don't pretend they do not exist.
	Avoid using qualifiers that reinforce stereotypes such as "We would hire women and people of color if they had skills."
	Refrain from speaking more loudly when communicating with individuals whose English is limited. Instead, try to speak more slowly and to pronounce each syllable. But don't do so unduly, or you will inadvertently be offensive.
	Use words that are gender neutral and recognize both genders (e.g., salesperson versus salesman, supervisor versus foreman, etc.).
	Use a wide variety of metaphors, analogies, and references, rather than just sporting or military expressions for instance.
	Be patient. It may take longer for a person whose native language is not English to process the information. Put yourself in their situation (e.g., traveling to their country where you have limited or no language understanding. Would you want and need time to process what you heard to create your response?).

(continued)

Figure 7-1. Effective Communication Tips to Work Productively Together *(concluded)*

✓	Key Ideas
	Use "I" messages as an assertive, culturally neutral way of saying that certain behavior is causing you difficulty, but that nonetheless you respect the rights of others.
	Be aware of your body language, that is, your non-verbal cues.
	Rephrase and say your message again if you feel you are not being understood. Use pictures and diagrams, when appropriate. Frequently ask open-ended questions to check for the other person's understanding.
	When listening, find ways to acknowledge the speaker's emotional state. It is helpful to give them your attention and watch for cues. Don't make assumptions. Ask for clarification if you sense a perceived frustration. Check to be certain you are hearing them correctly.

Dealing with Cross-Cultural Conflict

No matter how effective you are at communicating, when working in a diverse work team, conflicts will arise. Some conflict is healthy and promotes growth, learning, and understanding. The key is how you *handle* the conflict situation. Creative sparks can fly whenever diverse ideas and perspectives "rub against one another." Many of us have been trained through our cultural programming to avoid at all costs the unpleasantness of conflict. One of the keys to forming a diverse, high-performing team will be your ability to teach both managers and team members how to view conflict in a positive light and use it constructively, that is seize "a teachable moment." Some of the potential benefits of productive conflict are listed in Figure 7-2.

Figure 7-2. Benefits of Managing Cross-Cultural and Cross-Difference Conflict

✓	Key Ideas
	Creates a heightened sense of awareness of the problems that exist and the approaches needed or used to solve them.
	Gets people to consciously consider problems and novel solutions, rather than to just allow these problems to percolate away beneath the surface.
	Promotes a greater awareness of the "isms" of discrimination and creates a determination to eliminate them (if the team has been effectively trained to do this).
	Creates a heightened sensitivity toward the needs, styles, values, frustrations, and resentment of others.
	Generates an open expression of opposing views to critique old reasoning processes and develop new decision-making tools.
	Energizes people to use their root cause analysis skills to openly get to the heart of the matter.
	Helps the team take responsibility to be accountable to each other and improve morale.

(continued)

Figure 7-2. Benefits of Managing Cross-Cultural and Cross-Difference Conflict *(concluded)*

✓	Key Ideas
	Helps motivate members to come up with and articulate new solutions. Fosters creative risk-taking skills.
	Decreases costs by increasing efficiency to address problems in a direct, timely fashion.
	Improves customer relations and market penetration by addressing real needs and concerns.
	Reduces the organization's potential legal exposure.

When conflict does arise, it can be debilitating if it is not handled correctly. If your diverse work team is to work together productively, it will require a well-heeled process of communication, trust, and respect among team members. These situations can get even more complicated when the team has a broad mix of people who have different first languages. The solution requires that all members of the team have both self-awareness and cultural awareness. Any time diversity is added to a team, it changes the dynamics of the group. Through self-assessment and team analysis, you and your diverse work team can identify where cultural and other barriers can impair a team's performance and build strategies to work productively together.

References

Fernandez, J. P. (1999). *Race, gender and rhetoric*. New York: McGraw-Hill.

Hubbard, E. E. (2002). *Techniques for managing a diverse workforce*. Petaluma, CA: Global Insights Publishing.

Myers, S. G. (1996). *Team building for diverse work groups*. Irvine, CA: Richard Chang and Associates.

Chapter 8
Diversity and Organizational Change

Introduction

Effectively managing diversity requires that you be an effective manager of change. After all, diversity is not a program, "it is a process of systemic organizational change." When people think of diversity as a program, they might think that at some point they will be finished with it and can go on to something else. However, this is not the case. Generally speaking, the need to successfully manage diversity will always be a priority whenever you have people in the organization who are different in a variety of ways.

Like any other change initiative in the organization, to achieve results, your efforts to manage diversity in your workforce will require the basics of building a strategy, creating a tactical plan, taking ownership, being accountable, and implementing and measuring progress against the plan. It must also embody the principle of continuous improvement to seek new ways to create a high performing work environment using diversity.

Building a Change Strategy for Diversity Management

Developing a strategy and putting a plan in place are the first steps in any change effort. What separates an ordinary manager from a great manager of diversity is their ability not only to plan, but their ability to *execute* the plan, measure progress, make adjustments, and achieve results. Without these actions, even the best plans for change can fail.

To begin, it is critical that you create a personal action plan that focuses on the use of tools and techniques mentioned in this guidebook for diversity management.

Creating a Tactical Diversity Management Plan for Change

Once your diversity management strategy is in place, it is time to consider what is needed to create a set of tactical plans to put your diversity process into action. Initiating, changing, refocusing, or revitalizing your organization's commitment to create a diverse and inclusive environment starts with building a baseline—building a solid understanding of the organization's current level of effectiveness in mastering the basics that influence the organization's ability to lead and accelerate the diversity change process. This requires that you help the organization do the following:

❖ Analyze its communications strategy and messages

❖ Find out the state of the organization from the line perspective

❖ Create measures and key performance indicators that provide feedback proactively, not reactively

❖ Analyze and evaluate all supporting organizational processes and practices

❖ Search for "low hanging fruit" as well as set a plan for the long-term

Analyze the Organization's Communications Strategy and Messages

Communicate, communicate, communicate. It is critical that the messages regarding diversity get out to the workforce. Therefore, it is vital to determine how effectively you are communicating. Take the time to find out. Like any kind of change effort, a shift to a more diverse, inclusive work environment requires the leadership team to communicate the key themes of diversity consistently and often if it is to become a reality. Messages of diversity must be reflected in all the dimensions and language channels, which include words, behavior, and action. People within the organization must link diversity to the critical operating needs of the organization.

This won't happen using a pile of slides in a PowerPoint presentation or a slick model or card that states the organization's commitment to diversity. You, as a leader, must put your own signature on key diversity themes in "one-on-one" conversations, large and small group presentations, and your being visibly present to demonstrate your support. You should craft three or four themes that represent the key diversity messages you want to convey to your staff and others. What would you want to say to others that represents your values and commitment to create a diverse and inclusive organization? Use Exercise 8-1 to compile your themes.

Exercise 8-1. Key Diversity Themes I Support

Theme 1:_____

_____

What makes Theme 1 important to me and/or the organization?

_____

_____

_____

Messages I will deliver about this theme include:

_____

_____

_____

Theme 2:_____

_____

What makes Theme 2 important to me and/or the organization?

_____

_____

_____

Messages I will deliver about this theme include:

_____

_____

_____

Theme 3: _____

_____

What makes Theme 3 important to me and/or the organization?

_____

_____

_____

Messages I will deliver about this theme include:

_____

_____

_____

Theme 4: _____

_____

What makes Theme 4 important to me and/or the organization?

_____

_____

_____

Messages I will deliver about this theme include:

_____

_____

_____

Take the time to schedule the implementation of your diversity communications plan and the delivery of your key diversity messages (e.g., at the next staff meeting, in a one-on-one conversation, or during the next town hall meeting with your department or the organization). Think about the leaders and speakers who have had the most influence on you. What did they do to capture your attention and make their message stand out in your mind? Think about the fact that your audience will be made up of a diverse group of people, so you must think of the most effective way to communicate so that they are receptive.

In addition, be authentic. Your staff has heard you talk about things before and has judged you by it. If you have not been supportive of diversity previously, let them know what things led you to your current position and what they can count on you for in the future. Remember, everyone has the capacity to change if they really want to. You do not have to talk about what you did *not* do in the past. The past, including the good and the challenging, helped you to get to the point where you are today. And that includes gaining new knowledge about diversity and learning from it. Your messages must be delivered convincingly, consistently, and often, and you must be visibly supportive to effect change.

Find Out the State of the Organization from the Line Perspective

Creating a diverse organization with equal access at all levels and an environment that respects, values, and engages the talents of all its people does not happen or maintain itself automatically. It requires an ongoing strategic focus with systems, processes, values, and people to support it. Like any other change process, it takes time, conviction, and personal involvement. As a change agent and leader, you must get personally involved to ask "What's happening in our organization that supports diversity? What's not happening? What should I be doing right now to influence action toward our diversity vision? Toward the messages I support?" By taking time to assess where you are in the process, you open yourself up for the broader opportunities that might be available. You must model the inclusion process by getting others at all levels involved and working together productively toward the diversity vision.

Create Measures and Key Performance Indicators that Provide Feedback Proactively, Not Reactively

Compliance with laws and governmental regulations is only a small portion of what diversity is about. Diversity encompasses much, much more. Effective diversity performance and change is driven by execution, not by strategy alone, and diversity measurement drives execution.

It is a known fact that the best leaders accomplish their strategy by having goals and excellent feedback mechanisms to know they are making progress. They make it a point to personally inspect and find out how things are going. They use tools such as surveys, focus groups, town hall meetings, consultants, and steering committees to stay informed of the diversity change management process. They conduct informal reviews and check for problems. They create diversity metrics that are linked to the organization's strategy so that they know if the workforce is being fully utilized.

By working proactively instead of reactively, effective leaders are able to address issues before they become major problems. People respond to what is measured and reviewed. It helps to keep the diversity change effort focused and promotes continuous improvement.

Analyze and Evaluate All Supporting Organizational Processes and Practices

An effective diversity manager in a change process will search for leverage points—they look for influence points in other processes that help integrate diversity and inclusion into the organization's mainstream. They assess options and opportunities to enhance current organizational processes, so they include diversity supportive language, processes, and methods. This search for processes covers the gamut from operational processes and performance planning to work-life, customer strategies, and supply-chain management. Subtle messages and more overt processes for diversity and inclusion are a key part of the fabric that covers the way an organization does business.

Search for "Low Hanging Fruit" as well as Set a Plan for the Long-Term

In addition to creating a long-term, strategic approach, it is also important to recognize the things that are going well in the organization. Often, during your informal review, you will find people or diverse work teams doing outstanding work. Or, you may find opportunities for integrating diversity into the day-to-day process with little effort. Make it a point to seize these opportunities and recognize those who are making diversity happen in the organization.

In addition, spend some time consciously looking for areas that can be improved. Watch out for situations where employees might be receiving poor or mixed messages about the organization's commitment to diversity. Be sure to let employees know about your point of view and the key messages that are a part of your personal commitment. Leadership teams will be viewed as suspect if they talk favorably in public about diversity and building an inclusive work environment, yet make few efforts to be inclusive in their own interactions with people outside their inner circle. Here are a couple of contradictory diversity management practices to watch out for:

❖ Staff who talk about being friendly and welcoming to everyone, yet they are unapproachable and grumpy

❖ Managers who repeatedly cancel appointments, are late, or take calls when dealing with people who are different from themselves, yet this does not happen with their "inner circle" group

❖ Managers who consistently schedule meetings with weekend travel

❖ Managers espousing the value of diversity of thought and style, but who are quick to stamp out any new idea

What examples come to mind for you?

It is critical to remember that your strategies, measures, and messages are the basic fundamentals of change. It is up to you to plan your diversity change work and then work your plan!

References

Hubbard, E. E. (2002). *Techniques for managing a diverse workforce.* Petaluma, CA: Global Insights Publishing.

Chapter 9
Management Action Plan

Introduction

Effectively managing diversity requires commitment, planning, feedback, and accountability. It is critical that you develop a personal action plan to put what you have learned into action. Managing diversity successfully takes both awareness and action. But the action you take might vary according to the differences in your workplace. For example, cultural differences might require understanding and communication, while gender pay differential issues might require policy changes that must be implemented. The specific actions you take will depend on the issues, the expected outcome, your organization's need, the impact on your workforce, and above all, your commitment to diversity.

How Can You Improve?

Research and first-hand observation have taught us that diversity management competencies can be developed. If you really want to develop competency to improve your ability to manage diversity, the tools, information, and techniques in this pocket guide along with the following steps will get you off to a good start:

1. **Understand yourself.** Take a look at your scores on the Managing Diversity Profile. Compare your current level with where you would like to be.

2. **Understand the competency.** Study the behaviors and processes mentioned in this *Manager's Pocket Guide to*

Diversity Management. Make sure you understand what each competency area means, and identify the ways you could demonstrate the various behaviors.

3. **Practice the competency.** Focus on one or two competency areas at the most. Plan to use those behaviors as often as possible. Spend time deciding how you can use them. Start with behavioral changes that begin to stretch your thinking and work toward more challenging behaviors. The first time you try some of the behavioral changes, you might not succeed. It might also seem a little awkward. That's OK. Give yourself permission to fail once or twice.

4. **Get feedback.** You might not always be the best judge of your own diversity management competencies. Ask someone else to help you. Make it clear to the other person what you are trying to accomplish, and ask him or her to give you feedback on your progress. Or, ask them and others to assess your skill level by taking the 360° version of the Managing Diversity Profile (the Diversity Leadership Competency Profile). Alternatively, try to find a hard measure of your success, one that does not rely on your opinion. This step leads back to Step 1—understanding where you are now.

This guide is packed with diversity management information and several tools you can use. As you get more practice, your command of the diversity competency will improve—as long as you continue to get objective feedback on your performance to know where you stand. Some of the diversity management competencies are more challenging than others and might take much more time. Be sure to set realistic goals for yourself in terms of how quickly you will start to own the new behaviors and start to see change.

Figure 9-1 includes an action planning form. Complete the form for each competency area in which you would like to improve. The form asks you to make decisions about

❖ **Diversity Management Competency** (which Diversity Management Competency area you want to work on)

❖ **Your Improvement Goal** (the specific improvement objective you want to accomplish)

❖ **Action Items** (the specific steps and/or actions you will take to move your improvement efforts forward)

❖ **Measures of Success** (the evidence that will indicate you have succeeded)

❖ **Completion Dates** (the dates by which you will have completed the action items and achieved your goal)

❖ **Support** (someone to whom you can turn for coaching, advice, and encouragement, and getting feedback from others who are different from yourself)

Figure 9-1. Action Planning Form

Diversity Management Competency Area	Your Improvement Goal	Action Items	Measures of Success	Completion Dates	Support

Measuring Progress

There is an old saying that "you can't manage what you don't measure." Therefore, it is critical that you periodically measure your progress against the plan you create. During the process of individual and organizational change, it can be tempting to revert back to old habits and ways. Your old cultural programming software can creep back in, and reruns of old behavior might try to take over again.

It is crucial that you set up reinforcement processes and new patterns that take shape as current operating norms. Make it a point to meet with employees and ask "How are we doing as a diverse work team?" "If I could do one thing differently to make me even more effective as a diverse work team manager, what would you suggest I do?" "What is one thing that the organization can do differently to improve its diversity efforts overall?"

Get people together. Celebrate achievements with them. Develop a theme or focus based on the needs of your organization. At best, you will want to create an agenda that leads to an uplifting conclusion. Use that time as a forum to talk about specific challenges. Keep it positive by listening and acknowledging issues. Also engage people by encouraging them to participate in resolving key cross-cultural interaction and play a role in managing other key issues. It is important to let your team paint the picture of what diversity and inclusion will be like from their unique perspective and how it will contribute to making the organization better.

Walking the Talk

It takes a great deal of courage to understand, accept, and own up to your competency in managing diversity. It is easy to give up when things get tough or when it appears that diversity is no longer in vogue. It is easy to point fingers at others when the organization is not as welcoming to diversity as we would like it to be. Nonetheless, when we point fingers, at least three of our fingers point back. It is critical that you "walk your own talk." A lot will depend on what you do personally.

It is important to become conscious of what your own filters and personal biases are. You have to confront them and make certain you fully utilize the true gifts that your diverse workforce brings to the table. You can say all you want about your beliefs in diversity and inclusion, but if you don't take actions to prove it, people won't believe you.

Walking the talk means that you make certain you are living the diversity values standard you want or are holding others to meet. When you lead by example, employees get the message loud and clear that you not only talk about the importance of diversity, you live it by the way you interact with others. Modeling diversity leadership is critical for improved perform-ance using diversity. Remember, the net effect and impact of your behavior is multiplied over the number of lives you touch as a manager. You play a vital role in whether diversity in your organization is a reality or myth. I hope that you will choose to be the "difference that helps make the diversity difference!"

About the Author

Dr. Edward E. Hubbard is president and CEO of Hubbard & Hubbard, Inc., Petaluma, California, an international organization and human performance-consulting corporation that specializes in techniques for applied business performance improvement, workforce diversity measurement, instructional design, and organizational development.

He is the founder of the Hubbard Diversity Measurement and Productivity Institute and is also author of the following groundbreaking books: *Measuring Diversity Results, How to Calculate Diversity Return-on-Investment, Pathways to Diversity Metrics for Corporate Legal and Law Firms,* and four soon to be released books: *The Diversity Scorecard, The Diversity Performance Consultant's Fieldbook, Case Studies in Diversity Management and Measurement,* and *How to Develop a Measurable Diversity Strategic Plan.*

Dr. Hubbard is one of the first metrics authors in the field of diversity. As a result of his extensive research in the area of diversity measurement and expertise in computer programming, he is one of the first to develop automated software technologies for measuring diversity return-on-investment and performance improvements.

He has performed client work in organizational change and diverse workforce integration for private companies, the U.S. government, and corporate clients in the Far East and Pacific Rim. His work includes assisting organizations with staff development, quality improvement, performance improvement strategies, and restructuring work teams to utilize the strengths of a multi-ethnic workforce and handling diverse work group consolidations using self-directed work team and diversity return-on-investment measures and methods.

Dr. Hubbard is an internationally respected business consultant, trainer, and former professor and director at Ohio State University. He has served as a business professional at several Fortune 100 corporations such as Computer Systems Analyst, Informatics Corporation, Computer Room Operations Manager, Battelle Memorial Institute, Internal Consultant, and Mead Corporation. In addition, he has held the position of Director of Training and Organization Development for the $17 billion McKesson Corporation.

Recently, Dr. Hubbard received double honors; he has been named to the prestigious Who's Who in Leading American Executives and Who's Who Worldwide of Global Business Leaders. Memberships are limited to those individuals who have demonstrated outstanding leadership and achievement in their occupation, industry, or profession. Author of more than 37 books, Dr. Hubbard's other book titles include: *The Hidden Side of Employee Resistance to Change, Managing Customer Service on the Frontline, Managing Your Business for Profitable Growth, Hiring Strategies for Long-Term Success, How to Start Your Own Business with Empty Pockets,* and *Managing Organizational Change: Strategies for Building Commitment.*

Articles by Dr. Hubbard have appeared in magazines and newspapers such as *Inc., Fortune, Cultural Diversity at Work, Next Step Magazine, Forbes, American Society for Training and Development Journal, Sonoma Business Magazine, Organization Development Network Journal, The Cleveland Plain Dealer, The Press Democrat,* and *The Diversity Factor Magazine.* He has also been featured in several business films, in management development videos, and on radio programs. He is a regularly featured speaker and keynote for national and international conferences, teleconferences, seminars, and workshops.

Dr. Hubbard is an expert in organizational behavior, organizational analysis, applied performance improvement and measurement strategies, strategic planning, diversity measurement, and organizational change methodologies.

Dr. Hubbard earned Bachelor's and Master's Degrees from Ohio State University and earned a Ph.D. with Honors in Business Administration.

About the Hubbard Diversity Measurement and Productivity Institute

"Creating Applied Sciences for Measuring Diversity Performance and Results"

Hubbard & Hubbard, Inc., has established the Hubbard Diversity Measurement and Productivity Institute (DM&P) to provide measurement skills, certification workshop, and applied learning conferences for assessing, measuring, and evaluating diversity results in organizations.

Based on the ground-breaking book *Measuring Diversity Results* by Dr. Edward E. Hubbard, this institute is dedicated to assisting practitioners and other professionals with tools and techniques to research and develop measurable diversity business processes as well as case examples for diversity that clearly demonstrate impact on the financial bottom line of the organization. Our mission is to provide the most up-to-date tools that diversity professionals need to make effective, timely decisions in order to create a measurable performance impact. Sample workshop titles include:

❖ Measuring Diversity Results

❖ Building a Measurable Diversity Strategic Plan

❖ How to Calculate Diversity Return-on-Investment

❖ Building a Diversity Measurement Scorecard

❖ Creating and Implementing a Diversity Culture and Systems Audit

❖ How to Construct a Diversity Business Case

❖ Conducting a Cultural Due Diligence Audit

❖ Measuring Supplier Diversity Utilization

❖ Assessing Diversity Training Impact

❖ Creating Measures for Diverse Work Team Productivity

❖ Measuring Diversity Results: An Executive Overview

In addition, the Diversity Measurement and Productivity Institute (DM&P) offers a wide range of diversity productivity workshops for employees, managers, and executives such as:

❖ Diversity in the Workplace

❖ Diversity Leadership Skills

❖ Communicating across Cultures

❖ Supervising a Diverse Workforce

❖ Diversity Leadership Skills for Executives

Products available through the Diversity Measurement and Productivity Institute (DM&P) to support your diversity management skills include:

❖ Diversity Leadership Competency Profile—Full 360° version

❖ The Diversity Baseline Audit

❖ The Diversity 9-S Framework Audit

❖ Managing Expectations Survey

❖ The Diversity Climate Analysis

❖ MDR Express Checkup Software

❖ MDR Stat Pak 1 Software: Diversity Measurement Scorecard Startup Metrics

❖ MDR Stat Pak 3 Software: Measuring Diversity Staffing and Recruitment Impact

The Diversity Measurement and Productivity Institute (DM&P) also offers a full range of Diversity Certification Courses that result in two primary certifications for internal practitioners:

❖ Certified Internal Diversity Trainer

❖ Certified Internal Diversity Advisor

Please visit our Web site at www.HubbardNHubbardInc.com for more information and schedules.

Index